FINDING GOD TODAY

One Catholic's Way

E. Springs Steele

Paulist Press
New York/Mahwah, N.J.

Cover design by Cynthia Dunne

Library of Congress Cataloging-in-Publication Data
   Steele, E. Springs.
   Finding God today : one Catholic's way / E. Springs Steele.
     p. cm.—(IlluminationBook)
   Includes bibliographical references (p.   ).
   ISBN 0-8091-4326-7 (alk. paper)
   1. Spiritual life—Catholic Church. I. Title. II. IlluminationBooks.

BX2350.3.S74 2005
248.4'82—dc22

                                  2005001952

Published by Paulist Press
997 Macarthur Boulevard
Mahwah, New Jersey 07430

www.paulistpress.com

Printed and bound in the United States of America

Contents

"Again, the kingdom of heaven is like a merchant in search of fine pearls; on finding one pearl of great value, he went and sold all that he had and bought it."

(Matt 13:45–46)

Introduction

> *"Our hearts rest not, O Lord, until they rest in you."* —St. Augustine
>
> *"I was lookin' for love in all the wrong places."* —Johnny Lee
>
> *"Everybody's got a hungry heart."* —Bruce Springsteen

One of God's greatest gifts to me has been the luxury of a vocation given to teaching about finding God in everyday life. What I am discovering, however, is how difficult this search is for my students. I think there are several related reasons for this situation.

First, the religious culture (mid-twentieth century Catholic) in which I was nurtured is rapidly disappearing. I can no longer presume that my students have the theological language or "database" that I gained from memorizing the *Baltimore Catechism* and living in a world of Latin Masses, Gregorian chants, May processions, meatless

Fridays, midnight liturgies at Christmas and Easter, family prayer, and parochial school.

Second, the culture we do live in tells us that what is real is limited to what can be known through our senses. We have lost what Madeleine L'Engle calls *second sight,* "that gift which allows us to peek for a moment at the world beyond ordinary space and time."[1]

Our culture also tells us that we can only be satisfied, made whole, by that which can be bought and consumed. So shopping has replaced prayer, acquiring has replaced sacrifice, and consuming has replaced resting in the ever-deepening mystery of God's beauty and truth.

And finally, religion and spirituality have become "commodified." We live in a spiritual shopping mall. The religious treasures of many traditions and cultures are available at Borders; Amazon.com; a dizzying number of Web sites; and workshops, seminars, and retreats beyond enumeration. And while we are hungry for them, as witnessed by book sales, workshop sign-ups, and the mushrooming of businesses dedicated to servicing our spiritual needs, how do we know what to choose? Is it simply a matter of style, fit, and taste, like selecting a new dress or bottle of wine? Or do we have to be concerned about quality? Are some of these harmful or dead-ends?

Given this situation, it is difficult to know where to seek reliable, effective, practical methods for spiritual growth. And this is the case even for those of us who are fortunate to have such methods in our religious tradition, given the rapidly disappearing world that was their means of transmission. So what I seek to do is revisit basic forms of spiritual practice found in Roman Catholicism, and present them in an understandable way. But a few words of caution are necessary.

First, none of these methods are quick fixes. There are no shortcuts. There is nothing like the diets and exercise videos and machines we see on TV that promise beautiful bodies in no time, with little effort, discipline, or sacrifice required, or investment programs and franchises that offer the heaven of wealth tomorrow, for only a small fee. No, sorry. There's nothing like that in Catholic spirituality.

But what this tradition does tell us is that with the discipline of daily practice, our efforts to find and deepen our experience of God will lead us to the happiness and satisfaction that are our hearts' true desire. But this journey requires us to train our mind, heart, will, and imagination in a very special way. Thankfully there are a number of very practical methods of spiritual growth that provide just what we need. I will present a number of these, all related, in what follows.

Conceptual Foundation

There are several fundamental assumptions that undergird the Catholic spiritual tradition. The first is the presumption that there is more to us than we consciously know, and more to the world than what our senses tell us. A good word to summarize this assumption is *mystery*. It is to be understood in the sense of an infinite depth, often hidden, the experience of which takes us out of our ordinary self and into sacred time *(kairos)* and sacred place *(temenos)*.

To see, hear, feel, taste, or touch this mystery feels like coming to our true home, and is the answer to the hunger hinted at in the introductory quotes. It is where we meet God. In a very real sense it is an experience or revelation of heaven, and is something we all know. Haven't we each had a glimpse of a beauty that is deeper than the visual impressions of a sunrise or a gliding pelican on our corneas, or the sonic impressions of Gregorian chant on our eardrums? And haven't we perhaps understood a truth far beyond the words on a page of Tolkien or Merton or the Bible, a truth that takes us beyond words or concepts? Or known the deep mystery of life in the first cry of our just-born child, or the last breath of a parent who has lived and died courageously?

But my experience over the years has been that these moments of second sight, as Madeleine L'Engle calls them, often go unrecognized. Let me offer an example. Not so long ago one of my students came to me with a serious concern. He was troubled that as a "cradle" Catholic he felt that he had never had a religious or spiritual experience. So I asked him if he had ever had an experience that stood out in his memory as being particularly special, or real, an experience that made the rest of life seem like being asleep in comparison, an experience of great clarity or beauty. As I finished, he thought for a moment, and said that it was really strange that I asked. Three months earlier, just after Thanksgiving, he had been out hunting. The woods were beautiful. He sat down under a pine tree late in the afternoon and fell asleep. When he awoke, the ground was white with snow and the shadows were growing long with the approach of evening. It was so quiet he said he could hear the snow falling through the needles of the pine. There was a squirrel on the end of a log two feet from his feet, gathering nuts. And then he heard church bells in the distance from the valley. The tune was "O Holy Night." He sat for a moment after he had recounted the event. Then I could see the moment of his realization, the moment he connected this most special experience with the word *holy*. He turned to me, smiled, and said, "Thanks." And I thanked him for letting me be there with him.

Now for this student, that particular moment in that particular place became a gate to heaven, a moment where the veil was lifted, where he saw what is always there, when he tasted the real presence of God, where he communed with God under the appearance of nature. That particular moment and place became holy. And he could always return, at least in memory, and step outside of ordinary time and space into sacred time and space. And he could begin to recognize that presence at other times and places in his life.

In my own life there was a similar moment, one that marked me forever. I was thirteen or fourteen. Home was 1165 Partridge Road in Spartanburg, South Carolina. I woke up one spring Saturday morning feeling totally refreshed. I looked out my window at the yellow-green just-born leaves, the first hint of color on dogwoods and azaleas, smelled wisteria and honeysuckle, and luxuriated in the early morning sun streaming through it all. I felt such a sense of being unconditionally loved and simple joy-filled peace that I knew in the deepest part of myself that what my parents and church called God was real, and that this reality nurtured and sustained me even when I failed to see, hear, taste, touch, feel its vital presence. It was that moment that enlivened my faith, and rooted the Christian story into the essence of my being, even though it would take me many years and many trials to realize it.

But these experiences didn't come to me, and don't come to any of us, as the result of our own striving alone, like losing weight or reducing debt. They come to us feeling more like gifts (grace) than personal achievements. So the insight here is that coming to this experience of depth, fullness, richness, the experience of mystery where we meet God, where ordinary places and times are transfigured into sacred times and places, actually requires both our effort and God's. Work and grace are both necessary. And what we can do, perhaps the only thing, is to train ourselves to recognize the gift when it is offered and then choose to accept it. The rest is God's grace.

These two poles of spiritual growth, what I do and what God does, are fundamental to Catholic spiritual practice. To experience mystery, to enter our *kairos* and *temenos*, to have a moment of *revelation* or *transfiguration*, requires an ever-changing interplay of human effort and response to divine grace.

This dynamic aspect of spiritual growth is not exclusive to Roman Catholicism. In fact, the two poles have been beautifully named in Japanese Buddhism as *jiriki* and *tariki*. *Riki* means power. *Ji* means self and *ta* means other. So *jiriki* is self-power and *tariki* is other-power, or in Catholic language, my work and God's grace.

This dynamic tension is also a feature of the process of artistic creation. As Madeleine L'Engle says:

> The artist is a servant who is willing to be a birthgiver. In a very real sense, the artist (male or female) should be like Mary who, when the angel told her that she was to bear the Messiah, was obedient to the command....If the work comes to the artist and says, "Here I am, serve me," then the job of the artist, great or small, is to serve (*jiriki* in the terminology I've introduced)....When the work takes over (*tariki*, my terminology), then the artist is enabled to get out of the way, not to interfere. When the work takes over, the artist listens. But before he listens, paradoxically, he must work....We must work every day, whether we feel like it or not, otherwise when it comes time to get out of the way and listen to the work, we will not be able to heed it.[2]

This concept of "serving the work" is a wonderful way of understanding the process of spiritual growth, because, as L'Engle herself points out, "To serve a work of art is almost identical with adoring the Master of the Universe in contemplative prayer."[3] We work, then we let go. We practice our scales, learn our song by heart, and then let go and let the music flow through us. We pray, and then let God's mysterious love flow into us and through us to others. And when we do, we become co-creators, co-artists, with God, of the story of our life. As Thomas Merton wrote, "Our vocation is not simply to be, but to work together with God in the creation of our own life, our own identity, our own destiny."[4] To summarize briefly, the Catholic spiritual tradition presumes a depth to self and all reality that can be designated *mystery*. The human desire, dissatisfaction, or restlessness articulated in the quotes at the beginning of this Introduction is seen in the Catholic spiritual tradition as a deep, often unconscious, hunger to experience this mystery, which is its only satisfaction. To find satisfaction, to experience the revelation of this *foundational mystery*, is a process of human effort and response to divine grace, *jiriki* and *tariki*, serving the work, wherein we enter sacred time and place, becoming co-creators with God. In chapter one I will present three related practices leading to this experience of mystery: spiritual reading, *lectio divina*, and Ignatian mental prayer. Chapter two will then describe a systematic approach to praying the Rosary as a fourth way to serve the work. Chapters three and four are brief exercises that introduce chapter five's presentation of eucharistic liturgy (Mass) as a fifth means of making myself available for the experience of God's grace. The final chapter, chapter six, will offer specific suggestions for incorporating the fruit of spiritual practice into one's daily life.

CHAPTER ONE
Three Ways to Get Started

*T*he first three spiritual practices that I will present are connected. They are each based on reading texts. In the first, spiritual reading, we may choose any text. In the second, lectio divina, the traditional text is the Bible. And in the final practice, Ignatian mental prayer, the primary focus is on the four Gospels of the New Testament. I turn now to the description of each.

Spiritual Reading

As adults, perhaps our professional education and knowledge has outstripped our knowledge of God.

Although we may have very sophisticated understandings of the physical universe, human psychology, business and economics, law, medicine, and the arts, our theology can be that of a twelve year old. And this presents a problem in deepening our experience of God. How can we love someone we don't know?

To remedy this deficiency, we can dedicate ourselves to deepening our understanding of God. How? Nothing mysterious or mystical is involved. In fact, it may sound boring. We simply dedicate thirty minutes a day, at a regular time and place, to reading texts that open our minds and hearts to God. This is our work, *jiriki*.

Now, while books that are effective for me might not work for you, there are some tried-and-true favorites. One is Viktor Frankl's *Man's Search for Meaning*. Although written by a Jewish psychiatrist as a result of his time spent in Nazi concentration camps, it offers a most helpful perspective on faith that is consistent with Catholicism. Three other autobiographical accounts that many have found richly rewarding are Augustine's *Confessions*, Thomas Merton's *Seven Storey Mountain*, and Walter Ciszek's *He Leadeth Me*. The works of Anglican C. S. Lewis are also widely used, especially his *Screwtape Letters*, *The Problem of Pain*, and *The Great Divorce*. Dorothy Day's *The Long Loneliness* and Mother Teresa's *No Greater Love* should appeal to those of us oriented to action in the world on behalf of others, while Sidney Callahan's *With All Our Heart and Mind* is an exceptional presentation of spiritual counseling and comforting. Working through the *Catechism of the Catholic Church*, the second edition of

Monika Hellwig's *Understanding Catholicism*, or Luke T. Johnson's *The Creed* can be fruitful for the more analytically inclined. For others, artistically or aesthetically inclined, Thomas Merton's *New Seeds of Contemplation*, the poetry of Jesuit Gerard Manley Hopkins or Madeleine L'Engle's *Walking on Water* can open new vistas on the mystery of self, God, and world.

Such reading becomes spiritual practice by beginning with the simple intention of offering the time spent in reading to God. We then ask the Lord to open, inspire, or enlighten our understanding of the text. This is technically called *intercessory prayer*, and is a request for grace, for *tariki*. We then conclude with a simple prayer of thanksgiving, and a firm intention of applying what we have learned or been shown in our reading to the next twenty-four hours of our life. Such application is our work *(jiriki)*, but we are asking God for help (grace, *tariki*) in carrying it out. Done consistently, the effect can be like putting on those 3-D glasses we got at the movies when we were young. A whole new dimension (mystery, second sight) of life is revealed. And the only thing necessary on our part is consistency of practice and application of what is learned *(jiriki)*. God does the rest *(tariki)*.

Lectio Divina

A more focused version of spiritual reading is called *lectio divina*. It has a very long history in the Church. In simplest terms, *lectio divina* (sacred reading) is focusing one's spiritual reading on the Bible. To use this practice effectively, however, there are several preliminary things to understand: the nature of the Bible, coming to quiet, and experiencing God as word.

The Nature of the Bible

The Bible is a collection of diverse texts originally written in Hebrew, Aramaic, and Greek thousands of years ago in a culture very different from our own. So unless we choose to learn these languages, we will have to choose a translation. The two most often used by Catholics are the New American Bible and the New Revised Standard Version (used exclusively in this book). Having chosen our translation, it is necessary to take into consideration our degree of comfort reading these texts. This depends on our particular religious and educational background. While in many cases the basic message is clear, there are instances where background information is very helpful. Many Bibles provide such information in introductions to the individual books, cross-references, and footnotes to the text. But if we are truly serious about moving from spiritual reading to *lectio* it is very helpful to have access to commentaries appropriate to our level of familiarity with scripture, and that are suited to its use in this practice. If we are relative newcomers to the Bible, Father Lawrence Boadt's *Reading the Old Testament*, and Pheme Perkins' *Reading the New Testament* (second edition) are excellent general introductions. *The Collegeville Bible Commentary* is a two-volume set that offers informed but nontechnical commentaries on the individual books of Old and New Testaments.   '

Coming to Quiet

A second necessity, a very practical one, is finding a quiet place free from the possibility of interruption. For some of us, this may be the greatest challenge. There is also a real value in praying in the same place at a regular time. This creates a sacred place *(temenos)* and moment *(kairos)* for our coming to the Lord. With regular practice, simply coming to this place and time will bring us into the presence of mystery, second sight, God's presence.

Having found a quiet place, we need to come to inner quiet. This can be a real challenge. We live in a world that is filled with relentless appeals to each sense—sight, sound, taste, touch, and smell. We also live in a culture that urges us to move rather than sit, produce rather than appreciate, and do rather than simply be. So trying to come to inner quiet can feel like trying to brake a speeding car on an icy road. We try to come to inner quiet, only to discover that we are restless and guilty about all the practical things we should be doing. Or we become aware of physical aches and pains that distract us, or the million thoughts that simply will not disappear.

This is to be expected. It is the typical experience of all who seek the felt presence of God within. And there are a number of practical techniques for coming to interior quiet, of coming to be completely present in the present moment. I will present two.

Attention to Breath

One simple, standard method of developing the ability to concentrate is by attention to our breathing. It is most helpful if we can find a comfortable posture that keeps our back straight, and then breathe from our diaphragm rather than from our chest. What this means literally is that we push our stomach out to breathe in, and relax it to exhale. To come to interior quiet, we simply put attention on the rising and falling of breath either at the nostrils, back of the throat, or stomach. It is helpful to vocally or subvocally say "in" with the inhalation, and "out" with the exhalation. Simply feel the breath, and let go of all else. When a thought, feeling, or sensation distracts us, we don't become upset. Maintaining equanimity, we simply return our attention to the inflow and outflow of breath. This is an art, something only learned by regular practice, *jiriki*. If we are distracted 100 times, we return to attention to breath 101 times. Begin with a short period of practice and gradually extend it. Start with one minute, and gradually work to twenty minutes.

Daily Journaling

A second practice for coming to inner quiet is daily journaling. Sometimes there is too much going on in my life for attention to breath to be effective. If that is the case, I open a journal or notebook and write. It doesn't matter about content. I write to God or myself or the person that is my greatest love or hate. I write for twenty minutes at the same time of day, every day. This has the effect of clearing my mind and heart of major issues and distractions that take me out of presence to the present moment. It is a very practical means of concentration and recollection (re-collect attention). It is *jiriki,* making myself available.

Once we have come to quiet by either method, we remind ourselves that it is a very wonderful thing that we are about to begin, seeking the presence of the Lord in the text of scripture, and we ask God to bless this time and allow us to find God's presence in what we read. We may do this with a traditional formal prayer like "Come Holy Spirit":

> Come Holy Spirit, and fill the hearts of your faithful, and enkindle in them the fire of Your Love. Send forth Your Spirit, and they shall be created, and You shall renew the face of the earth. O God, Who by the light of your Holy Spirit instructed the hearts of the faithful, grant, that by that same Spirit we may be truly wise and ever rejoice in His consolation. We ask this through Christ our Lord. Amen.

Or we may choose a prayer we have developed ourselves or a spontaneous prayer from our heart. Beginning with such prayers creates an attitude of mind and heart that is most conducive to serving the work.

Finding God in Scripture:
Experiencing God as Word

Now this last preparatory step, praying to find God's presence in scripture, may sound odd. After all, isn't the Bible God's word? Well, yes, of course. But there is a much deeper sense of the term *God's word*. Let me explain. When we speak, our words are our attempt to communicate thoughts and feelings to others. Sometimes we are very successful, and at other times less so. Now if we chose the perfect words, they would communicate exactly what we are thinking and feeling. In an important way, our words would be our thoughts and feelings, would incarnate (enflesh) our thoughts and feelings, and reveal who we are. But we are human, and can rarely do this to perfection.

With God it is different. According to the first chapter of the Bible, God creates by speaking: "Then God said, 'Let there be light'; and there was light" (Gen 1:3). God's word is totally efficacious; it brings into perfect existence what it names. And what God first brought into being was the created world. It was God's first word to us, and insofar as words reveal the speaker, creation is God showing us God, God revealing God to us in much the same way an artist reveals herself in her art.

But according to the Bible, we humans had some difficulty in hearing God's word in creation clearly. So God's next attempt was more explicit. He revealed himself to Abraham and then to Moses, and his word was in the form of laws *(torah)*. In fact, the Ten Commandments are commonly referred to as the Decalogue, the Ten Words. So *torah* was God's second word of revelation.

But we still had difficulty hearing. So God spoke God's word through the prophets, and yet again human response was less than perfect. So, from a Christian standpoint, God decided that the only way to get through to us was to enter into our condition, become one of us. So God's final word to us, which is the perfect expression of the being and will of God and therefore God also, took on flesh in the person of Jesus of Nazareth. As the beginning of the Gospel of John puts it:

> And the Word became flesh and lived among us, and we have seen his glory, the glory as of a father's only son, full of grace and truth. From his fullness we have all received, grace upon grace. The law indeed was given through Moses; grace and truth came through Jesus Christ. No one has ever seen God. It is God the only Son, who is close to the Father's heart, who has made him known. (John 1:14, 16–18)

So Jesus is God's perfect revelation, perfect "word" to us. And the Bible contains this word, in the words of humans. In the Bible, we can have direct contact with this living word of God, who is God. And that is the ultimate goal of *lectio divina.* As Michael Casey puts it:

...authentic *lectio,* far from being exposure to mere words, is a means of setting aside the superficial to reach the heart of reality. It is the search for the unique Word of God, who lies beneath and beyond the multiplied words of human beings.[1]

Thus we can come into contact with the living reality of the word, the second person of the Trinity, as truly in *lectio* as in the consecrated bread and wine of the Eucharist. And that is the ultimate purpose of this form of practice. So now to the "how to."

The Method of *Lectio Divina*

Traditionally there are four steps in the practice of *lectio:* reading the text *(lectio),* analyzing the text *(meditatio),* praying from the text *(oratio),* and resting in or savoring the experience of the word *(contemplatio).* Each will be treated in turn.

Reading

The first task is to choose an appropriate biblical text. There are several general possibilities. One is to choose a favorite passage. Another is to use the readings of the Mass of the day (from the *Lectionary* and found listed in the *Ordo*). The last option, and the traditional choice, is to choose an entire biblical book and use it sequentially, daily, until its conclusion. Although knowledgeable writers on this method of prayer can be found who support each possibility, I think the best choice is using an entire biblical book. It allows us to really understand our daily reading in its literary and theological context, and works against reading our own meanings into scripture. And it encourages a reverent listening to the text. Good beginning choices are those books that don't require much background information to appreciate. In the Old Testament these would be the Wisdom writings, especially Psalms, Proverbs, the Song of Songs, Wisdom, and Sirach. In the New Testament, the Gospels of Mark and Luke, and the letters of Peter, James, and John are excellent initial books.

After choosing a text, it is important to begin by coming to quiet and offering an introductory prayer, just as you would do in the practice of spiritual reading. Then we begin to read in the same way that we would drink a $100 bottle of wine—slowly and with great appreciation. We bring to reading the perspective that this is God speaking to us in our life right now. Then we read until a word, phrase, or image hooks our attention. When this happens, it is time for the next phase, meditation. But one word of advice: some days nothing will attract us, and on other days it will be the first word we read. If the latter is the case, we stop reading and stay with the word or phrase or image until its attraction fades. Even if it takes days or weeks. Think of our attraction as a deep response to the word, to God speaking directly to us. On the other hand, if nothing has attracted us in the thirty minutes we have spent reading, don't be surprised if a word, phrase, or image pops into our mind or heart later in the day. If it does, we pay careful attention to what is going on at the time, and presume the text contains an important message or insight for us. These delayed revelations can also occur in dreams that night.

Meditation

When we have been hooked by the text, it is time to stop reading. It is time to allow our intellect and imagination and intuition, our head, to work on the compelling word, phrase, or image. What are the thoughts, feelings, and memories that come to mind in association with this text? What are the connections to our life, past, present, or future? It is often helpful to have a journal to jot down what comes to us at this point. Why? Because, as Thelma Hall puts it, this is when biblical "...words, events, etc., are prayerfully pondered and reflected on with the object of drawing from them some personal meaning or moral."[2] It is when our mind gains a deeper or broader understanding about God, self, and others. Then once our head is sufficiently nourished, it is time to turn to the heart phase, prayer.

Prayer

This phase of *lectio* is reached when our mind is sufficiently satisfied. We then turn to the Lord and speak from our heart about what we have learned, as simply and honestly as possible. Perhaps we are grateful for an insight, sorry about a failing, or feel some need. We put these feelings into words to God, expressing gratitude for this taste of the living word. We let the heart take over. And when the heart has said all it has to say, we take a deep breath, literally or figuratively, and simply come to rest. We have done all we can do. The *jiriki* is done. Let go, come to inner quiet, and simply let what comes, come. This is womb of mystery, revelation, contemplation. It is *tariki* time.

Contemplation

What is contemplation? Technically, it is the increasingly unfiltered experience of God found when we enter sacred time and sacred place. It is another term for the *tariki* experience of mystery. What the first three phases of *lectio* do is make us open, available, or vulnerable to this experience. They are collectively the *jiriki* aspects of this method. They lead to instances of contemplation, the *tariki* moments, spontaneous moments of grace, glimpses of glory and mystery, moments wherein the word touches our mind and heart directly.

When the contemplative moment ends, we then seek to take what has been experienced in this way of prayer and apply it to our daily life. We incarnate, enflesh, make visible, the gifts we have received. We serve the work. This application of the fruit of prayer to daily life locks in the transformation of mind and heart and imagination that has taken place in our time with God's word. And it accelerates our growth in intimacy with God. As we live from the experience of the word, we begin to see more deeply into self and others, and life in general. This deepened experience is then brought into our next daily *lectio*, and we will find ever more profound meaning in what is read. We begin to discover that scripture has a mysterious depth, and the deeper we go into self, God, and others, the deeper appreciation we have of the text. And all—self, God, others, and Bible—are gradually discovered to be bottomless. This bottomlessness of meaning and insight is yet another face of mystery.

We now turn to the third and final practice involving reading, Ignatian mental prayer.

Ignatian Mental Prayer

One of the clearest paths of spiritual practice to follow is that initiated by the founder of the Society of Jesus, St. Ignatius of Loyola, and developed over time by his order. Termed *mental prayer*, most simply it is bringing one's mind, either analytically or imaginatively, to an individual gospel text. This is a difference between it and *lectio*: *Mental prayer* has a narrower scope. *Lectio* has the entire Bible as a source for texts. By its exclusive focus on the Gospels, Ignatian mental prayer brings Jesus to the center of attention.

Choice of Gospel Text

The choice of a gospel text for Ignatian mental prayer is left to the individual. We may choose the gospel text for the current day's liturgy or for the upcoming Sunday liturgy. Or we may choose a favorite passage. For those unfamiliar with the Gospels, it may be helpful to know that the first three Gospels (Matthew, Mark, and Luke) have much material in common, while the fourth

Gospel (John) is relatively unique. And each of the four has a different flavor. Matthew's Gospel presents Jesus as the "new Moses," and has a focus on his teachings. There are many pithy sayings, the Sermon on the Mount, and the familiar Last Judgment passage where Jesus says, "Whatsoever you have done to the least of my sisters and brothers, you have done to me." Mark, on the other hand, focuses on the person of Jesus, and the effect he had on those that came into contact with him. It is fast moving, and offers a very human Jesus. Luke is written to non-Jews, and also puts Jesus' humanity in the foreground. In Luke, we see a Jesus who reaches out to the marginalized, and seems to have a special concern for women. And in John, there is an emphasis on the divinity of Jesus.

Choice of Mode

The choice between the analytic and imagination-based modes in Ignatian mental prayer is based on temperament. The analytic mode takes a text apart, seeking its message to us in our life right now. The imagination-based approach seeks to enter a gospel passage the way we read a good novel or view a great film. We become part of it, seeing the sights and smelling the smells, and come away changed by the experience.

At this point a note of explanation is necessary. The Ignatian tradition refers to the analytic mode as *meditation* and the imagination-based mode as *contemplation*. Both are understood to be *jiriki*. This is where confusion may occur. The *lectio* tradition uses the word *contemplation* to signify the *tariki* experience of grace while the Ignatian tradition uses it to signify the *jiriki* work of imaginatively entering a gospel text. So the two traditions use the same term, contemplation, in very different ways. To avoid confusion, I will use the term *imaginative reconstruction* instead of contemplation to designate the imagination-based mode of Ignatian mental prayer, while retaining the traditional Ignatian term *meditation* for the analytic mode.

Method

In treating the actual method of Ignatian mental prayer, I draw heavily on what Thomas Green has written in his wonderful book, *Opening to God.*[3] In it, Father Green indicates that regardless of one's choice of the analytic or imaginative approach, there are four steps in Ignatian mental prayer: remote preparation, immediate preparation, meditation or imaginative reconstruction, and colloquy. I will explain each by using a specific gospel passage, the story of a woman accused of adultery found in the Gospel of John (8:2–11).

> Early in the morning he came again to the temple. All the people came to him and he sat down and began to teach them. The scribes and the Pharisees brought a woman who had been caught in adultery; and making her stand before all of them, they said to him, "Teacher, this woman was caught in the very act of committing adultery. Now in the law Moses com-

manded us to stone such women. Now what do you say?" They said this to test him, so that they might have some charge to bring against him. Jesus bent down and wrote with his finger on the ground. When they kept on questioning him, he straightened up and said to them, "Let anyone among you who is without sin be the first to throw a stone at her." And once again he bent down and wrote on the ground. When they heard it, they went away, one by one, beginning with the elders; and Jesus was left alone with the woman standing before him. Jesus straightened up and said to her, "Woman, where are they? Has no one condemned you?" She said, "No one, sir." And Jesus said, "Neither do I condemn you. Go your way, and from now on do not sin again."

Remote Preparation

The first step in Ignatian mental prayer is termed the remote preparation. If we plan to pray over a particular text in the morning, then the night before we read it over. The purpose is twofold. The first is to make certain we understand the text, and the second is to plant it within ourselves. Let me explain both.

Concerning the first purpose, recall the consideration about the Bible made in reference to *lectio*. The

Gospels are texts originally written in Greek two thousand years ago in a culture very different from our own. We have varying degrees of comfort reading them, depending on our religious and educational backgrounds. Often the basic message is clear, but there are cases where background information is very helpful. Many Bibles provide such information in footnotes to the text.

If we have little experience in reading the Gospels, we might not know who the scribes and Pharisees were and their significance in the text. References to Moses and the law, the charges brought against the woman, the legal system and role of witnesses, and the meaning of Jesus writing in the dirt rather than replying immediately to his questioners also might be unclear. If such is the case, it is important to consult an appropriate gospel commentary. This is part of the personal effort, the *jiriki*, involved in beginning this type of prayer.

When we consult an appropriate commentary, we will discover that the scribes are a professional class. They know how to read and write, which most people did not know how to do in this essentially oral culture. They are the scholars, the intellectuals. The Pharisees, on the other hand, are a Jewish religious group. They are the ones who take the practice of their faith very seriously, both the ritual and moral aspects. In all four Gospels the scribes and Pharisees often appear together, and represent the best and brightest of religious Jews.

The obvious issue in our passage is the Law of Moses and what it says about adultery. All Jews (and remember that Jesus and the first Christians were all

Jewish) regarded the law *(torah)* as God's revealed will. It was the central feature of the covenant between God and Israel. Fidelity to it was called righteousness, and infidelity was called sin. So what does the law of Moses say about adultery? Depending on the situation, those convicted of adultery could be stoned to death. Conviction was based on the testimony of two witnesses, who according to Deuteronomy 17:7 were to throw the first stones. So on the face of it the scribes and the Pharisees are asking Jesus to demonstrate his faithfulness to God by condoning the woman's execution. But notice that in verse 6 the narrator suggests that it is really a trap.

When we have read the text carefully and are comfortable about its meaning, the remote preparation is finished. We now sleep on it, literally. We allow our unconscious mind an opportunity to work on it, thus fulfilling the second purpose of this initial preparation that was just noted, the planting it within oneself.

Immediate Preparation

The next step in Ignatian mental prayer is the immediate preparation. This is what we do immediately before either Ignatian meditation or imaginative reconstruction. The method is the same as for *lectio:* coming to exterior and interior quiet, and offering a formal or spontaneous prayer asking for enlightenment and acknowledging the marvelous thing we are about to do.

MEDITATION

The third and central element of Ignatian mental prayer is doing either the meditation or imaginative reconstruction. Looking at meditation first, we recall that this is the application of analytic reason to a gospel text. If we use the passage from John 8, the first step is to recall what we have learned from the remote preparation, and ask, "What does Jesus say and do, and what is the application to my own life?" We may also look at the other individuals in the text, and ask the same questions. Depending on what's going on in our life at the time of the meditation, we may naturally identify with Jesus, or the woman, or one of the accusers. If we identify with Jesus, we may be struck by how quickly he understands the motive of his accusers and how creatively he responds. He does not deny the validity of Mosaic Law or the truth of the charge brought against the woman. What Jesus does is humanize the situation. He invites the scribes and Pharisees to realize that they too are unfaithful to the *torah*, that they are sinners just like the woman. And in that moment of realization, each accuser turns and walks away. But the account doesn't end there. Jesus turns to the woman, addresses her directly, without accusation, but with the implicit recognition of her sinfulness. He says to her, simply, "Go your way, and from now on do not sin again." Jesus is the consummate moral teacher. Both accusers and accused have been touched. The lesson we may take away, beyond a deepened appreciation of Jesus' understanding of human nature and ability to bring about moral conversion, is an insight into the intimate relationship of justice and mercy. Speaking personally, I know myself that when I am called to make a moral judgment that I either feel a duty to go by the book or seek to avoid conflict and simply forgive or condone. Jesus does neither. He creates an opportunity where both the self-righteousness of the scribes and Pharisees and the moral failure of the woman are brought to the light of awareness, acknowledged, and transformed into deepened self-knowledge and moral growth. Perhaps we will realize that we are called to do the same.

It may be, however, that we more naturally identify with the woman than with Jesus. Perhaps we come to the text with a deep sense of guilt or shame about a recent misdeed or an ongoing weakness. Our self-esteem is very low, and we are defensive and hypersensitive, and know how others would judge us if they knew about it. We would expect the same treatment the woman receives from the Pharisees and scribes, and presume God judges us similarly. What a surprise we receive in the words and actions of Jesus. We sense unconditional love, gentleness, and feel his direct clear gaze into our heart. He seems to know us better than we know ourselves, and somehow doesn't hate us. In the experience of that love and affirmation, we can receive his gentle admonition to "Go your way, and from now on do not sin again." That is the message that we take away.

Perhaps the individual(s) we are least likely to identify with are the scribes and Pharisees. After all, they are the "bad guys" in the story. And self-righteousness is very difficult to recognize in process. It doesn't feel sinful. In fact, it feels just the opposite. Most times we see ourselves in the right. It is the other person who has clearly failed to measure up to whatever standard we are applying. And they deserve judgment. They eat, drink, or smoke too much. They don't work hard enough, exercise enough, or take care of their house, car, or kids properly. And, you know, that all may be true. But it is precisely this attitude that is self-righteousness. Notice that the Pharisees and scribes came in with it, but left without it. And this is perhaps the deepest meditation for those of us sincerely seeking God in prayer. After all, we are spending time and energy in something that requires real effort, and that is inherently good. And when we look around we see most people seeking the gods of contemporary American culture: wealth, fame, and power. How can we, even unconsciously, not be inclined to look down on them? The lesson here is that the only one without sin in the story, Jesus, didn't pick up the first stone. Perhaps when we are without sin, self-righteousness disappears. But until that is the case, we are called to become ever more sensitive to the sin of good people, our sin, the ingrained tendency to look down and judge others.

IMAGINATIVE RECONSTRUCTION

In Ignatian meditation, there is a certain distance between the text and oneself. With the second mode, imaginative reconstruction, there is no distance. We seek to enter the world of the scene the way we watch a compelling movie, read a can't-put-it-down novel, or sink into beautiful music. It is the difference between analyzing Shakespeare's *Romeo and Juliet* in a drama class, and seeing it performed live on stage in London.

Turning to our passage, what we seek to do is enter the scene with as many of our senses as possible. What is the time of day, weather, sights, smells, and sounds? What does Jesus look like, and the other characters as well? It is often helpful to become one of the crowd, and observe the scene as it unfolds. And sometimes it is a very powerful experience to let ourselves become one of the central characters. In doing this we allow our imagination great freedom. We don't have to follow the text slavishly. I offer the following as an example.

> *My name is Gamaliel. By profession I am a scribe, and by faith I am a Pharisee. I am the eldest of the Pharisaic scribes, and have lived my life seeking righteousness by following the Law of Moses. I now use my skills as a writer to record the most powerful experience of my life. My chronicle follows.*
>
> *Over the last months we in Jerusalem had heard accounts of a new teacher, a Galilean. According to the reports of many he had attracted great crowds, worked wonders, and taught powerfully. There were whispers that those close to him saw him as the Awaited One, the Messiah. And others said something even more troubling, that he claimed a unique relationship to the Holy One. So*

when he came to Jerusalem, and began to teach and attract crowds, I felt that it was my responsibility as eldest to determine his fidelity to the tradition of our people. One so popular could lead many astray.

The opportunity to test the young rabbi presented itself when a woman was accused of adultery. There were some irregularities concerning the witnesses, and the man involved was quite prominent. But nonetheless we decided it was the best chance we had to test this new teacher. We would bring the woman to him and ask him what should be done to her.

It was nearing midday, and the man Jesus was teaching a crowd. We gathered, prominent scribes and Pharisees, and took the woman with us. Although the law requires punishment of both parties involved, for reasons I thought prudent at the time we left the man out of it. As we approached, I saw a man of ordinary height and appearance holding the crowd spellbound. As I came closer, I noticed his seamless robe, his gentle but passionate tone, and above all, his eyes. Although not more that thirty years of age, his eyes were those of the holy elders. My heart told me that there was truth in the reports we had heard, but my life of devotion to the letter of the law required me to carry through on our plans to test the young rabbi's faithfulness to God's will as known through Moses.

The day was warm, and the sun painted the beautiful hills and walls of Jerusalem a brilliant white. We could smell the aroma of the market: fruits, vegetables, fish, and spices for sale. And the musky smell of donkeys and camels and the crowd in the midday heat was almost overwhelming. In the background we could hear the merchants trying to lure buyers to their booths. But in the midst of all this, the man Jesus held the crowd with his eyes and sonorous voice. And so we came to him.

The crowd backed away. We have their respect. We are scholars and on fire for strict adherence to the Law. None would dare stand in our way. I spoke.

"Teacher, this woman was caught in the very act of committing adultery. Now in the law Moses commanded us to stone such women. Now what do you say?"

I knew we had him in a predicament. If he said to carry out the sentence he would turn the crowd against him and incur the wrath of our Roman overlords, who alone have the authority to carry out such a punishment. And if he said to release the woman, he would have demonstrated that he does not observe the Law.

But he did not reply. He bent over, and began to write something in the dirt. I was not close enough to see what it was, but some of the other scribes did. And they appeared increasingly concerned. But I pressed him again to answer. And then came the words that overturned my world.

"Let anyone among you who is without sin be the first to throw a stone at her."

Jesus saw only the woman who was accused, and recognized the absence of her partner in sin. And I knew the witnesses were not with us, the only ones according to the Law who could cast the first stones. He had read our hearts, and knew our insincerity. And I stood accused myself, knowing the Law and having failed to observe it in this case. And he looked at me with those eyes. I could not withstand his gaze, and turned away in shame. All those with me did so as well. He knew the Law, almost as if he himself had written it. And he knew its spirit. He taught me the shallowness of my knowledge and practice, and my own sinfulness. But that was not the end of his lesson.

Although I turned away, I had to see how he treated the woman. I moved quietly to the back of the crowd. Jesus looked up at the woman and asked "Woman, where are they? Has no one condemned you?" She said, "No one, sir." And Jesus said, "Neither do I condemn you. Go your way, and from now on do not sin again." The lesson and my conversion were complete. Jesus knew the woman had broken the Law. He knew she had been scared to death by what we had done, and was ready to begin a new life. He spoke just the words she needed to hear. And it was as if he knew I was listening and watching as well. The words he spoke to her also spoke to the deepest part of my heart. Although he could have condemned me for my hardness of heart, my sinful self-righteousness, he didn't. And in the depth of my shame and guilt, I knew I would never again be quick to judge.

I hope this example gives a sense of the mode of Ignatian prayer that I have termed imaginative reconstruction. It might be helpful to read back through the meditation on this passage to appreciate the difference. Both approaches result in the same message, but one engages the analytic function of the mind while the other calls upon the imagination. In contemporary popular psychological terms, Ignatian meditation is left brained, and Ignatian imaginative reconstruction is right brained. Typically a person will find one easier than the other, although the more difficult can be the more fruitful. And it is good to change approaches from time to time.

Colloquy

The final part of Ignatian mental prayer, whether meditation or imaginative reconstruction, is a concluding heartfelt prayer of gratitude and resolution to carry the results into my daily life. It corresponds to the third aspect of *lectio*, the *oratio* (prayer). As an example, I offer the following:

> *Dear God, I am grateful to you for opening this scripture to me. It has given me a deeper appreciation of your Son, and my own frailty. I ask your grace to help me become especially conscious of judging others today, and resolve not to speak or act from such impulses, feelings, or thoughts. Amen.*

Notice that the colloquy brings the fruit of our meditation or imaginative reconstruction into our daily life. The results are the same as for *lectio*. And over time, the colloquy becomes the deepest element of this form of prayer. One moves more and more from head (reason or imagination) to heart. And when this begins to happen, rest easy. Simply allow the heart to find its home. *Jiriki* is over and we have begun to serve the work.

Ignatian mental prayer is thus a straightforward, systematic approach to deepening one's experience of God. It is initially cognitive, whether in its left brained (meditation) or right brained (imaginative reconstruction) mode. Over time it becomes increasingly affective, engaging the heart as well as the mind. It is also a wonderful way of deepening one's familiarity with Jesus and the Gospels.

The steps are simple: remote preparation (reading for comprehension, with biblical tools if necessary), immediate preparation (coming to quiet and setting the appropriate attitude through prayer), meditation or imaginative reconstruction (analysis or immersion), and colloquy (spontaneous prayer responding to the meditative or contemplative experience). Practiced over time it typically results in *lights* (spontaneous deep insights into scripture, self, others, situations) and *consolations* (spontaneous affective states of great joy, peace, faith, hope, and love). These are clearly *tariki* experiences. And with regular practice the initial feeling that we are doing all the work changes; we more and more serve the work. The time spent in prayer passes joyfully and too quickly. We also begin to become increasingly aware of the initial impulses behind our thoughts, words, and deeds, which gives us more freedom to act in a manner consonant with what we have learned in prayer. And often there is a surprising release from internal and external moral difficulties. It is a wonderful honeymoon with the Lord.

CHAPTER TWO
The Rosary

*A*s a Southern Catholic child of the fifties, one deep and comforting memory is saying the family Rosary before bed on warm summer evenings with the attic fan cooling the house. The hum of the fan, the movement of cool honeysuckle scented air, and the rhythmic repetition of "Hail Mary, full of grace..." was a wonderful way of moving into sleep.

This memory was resurrected in a very powerful way during another movement into rest. My father died on Easter Sunday 1989, a glorious azalea and camellia-filled morning in Charleston, South Carolina. Later in the week two of his closest childhood friends, Father Joe Murphy of the Diocese of Charleston and Father Ned Joyce, CSC, led all who had come to pay respects in the Rosary. It had been a long time since I'd been to a Southern wake, and the presence of family and friends whom I hadn't seen in a long while, together with the Rosary, brought me back home, both emotionally and spiritually. The comfort and support I felt were profound. It is a mark of the wisdom of our religious tradition to have developed a devotional practice that connects us so intimately to the Mother of God, about whom we believe, in the words of the *Memorare*, "...that never was it known that anyone who fled to your protection, implored your help, or sought your intercession was left unaided."

First Stage of Practice

I learned to say the Rosary at home. It wasn't that difficult, because it incorporated prayers that I already knew: the Apostles' Creed, Our Father, Glory Be, Hail Mary, and Hail Holy Queen. At home we simply said the prayers in the traditional order. It was rhythmic vocal prayer, *jiriki*. And that is the best way to begin. The key is daily practice. What we are seeking to do is become familiar and comfortable with the prayers and using the beads. And then we begin to see that saying the Rosary is a marvelous method for coming to quiet. A clear diagram with the text of each of the prayers is found in the Appendix. Said daily *(jiriki)*, the effects are identical to those resulting from Ignatian prayer. Lights and consolations *(tariki)* begin to grace our prayer, and there are very positive effects in our daily lives and relationships.

Second Stage of Practice

Background

Once we are comfortable with this level of practice, essentially coming to quiet through repetitive vocal prayer, it is possible to begin to transition into the next stage of the method. This next level of practice adds the announcement of a specific Gospel *mystery* to each decade. These mysteries are not mysteries of the faith but rather events or scenes in the life of Jesus and the Holy Family. They are called mysteries for historical rather than theological reasons. During the Middle Ages, most people were illiterate. Faith often was taught through art, especially stained glass and drama. Concerning the latter, "...religious plays were performed in public squares....These plays were called Miracle or Mystery plays. The word *mystery* was then applied to the Rosary because by our meditation we should 'picture' or imagine the mystery. This 'picturing' is like watching one of those Mystery Plays."[1]

So, the Rosary itself is a devotional practice that had its origin in the Middle Ages. The history is complex. For those interested, John Desmond Miller's *Beads and Prayers: The Rosary in History and Devotion* (Burnes and Oates, 2002) is an excellent source, and an abridged version can be found online.[2] Until October 16, 2002, there were three sets of mysteries: Joyful, Sorrowful, and Glorious. In his Apostolic Letter *Rosarium Virginis Mariae* dated October 16, 2002,[3] Pope John Paul II has suggested the addition of a fourth set, the Luminous Mysteries. His motive was to include events of Jesus' public ministry, as found in the Gospels, so that a person working through all four sets in their suggested order (Joyful, Luminous, Sorrowful, and Glorious), would visit the major moments in the Christian story of salvation. The following is a brief summary of each set.

The Joyful Mysteries highlight the beginning of the story up to the public ministry of Jesus: (1) the Annunciation of Gabriel to Mary, (2) the Visitation of Mary to her cousin Elizabeth, (3) the Nativity of Our Lord, (4) the Presentation of the infant Jesus in the Temple, and (5) the Finding of the adolescent Jesus in the Temple. The new Luminous Mysteries focus on the public life of Jesus prior to his Passion: (1) his Baptism by John, (2) the Wedding Feast at Cana, (3) his Proclamation of the Kingdom of God, (4) his Transfiguration, and (5) the first Eucharist at the Last Supper. The Sorrowful Mysteries are centered on Jesus' last day (Jewish, sunset to sunset): (1) the Agony in the Garden, (2) the Scourging at the Pillar, (3) the Crowning with Thorns, (4) the Carrying of the Cross, and (5) the Crucifixion. As the pope notes, the Sorrowful Mysteries "help the believer to relive the death of Jesus, to stand at the foot of the Cross beside Mary, to enter with her into the depth of God's love for man and to experience all its life-giving power."[4] And finally, the Glorious Mysteries focus on the Risen Christ: (1) the Resurrection, (2) Ascension, (3) Pentecost, (4) Assumption of Mary, and (5) the Coronation of Mary as Queen of Heaven and Earth.

Method

To move to the second level of practice, we simply announce or recall the appropriate mystery (scene, event) for each decade. For example, on Mondays and Saturdays, when the Joyful Mysteries are used, we simply start the first decade by saying, "the first Joyful Mystery, the Annunciation." Then we begin the second decade with, "the second Joyful Mystery, the Visitation," and so on. The diagram in the Appendix contains the individual mysteries and the days for each group.

Third Stage of Practice

Once we are comfortable with the simple announcement of the individual mysteries, it is possible to move to the third level of practice. Here one adds reading a brief scriptural text associated with each mystery. The traditional choices are found in the Appendix. Initially, we simply try to become comfortable reading (if praying individually) or listening (if praying in a group) to the chosen gospel text before each decade. Presuming the verbal repetition of the Hail Marys of each decade has become so comfortable that little conscious attention is required for that component of the devotion, it is possible to begin to shift attention to the individual mysteries while still saying the decade. We put attention to the mystery (scene, event) in the foreground of consciousness, and allow verbal recitation to sink to the background.

Now what does it mean to give attention to the gospel text? Let me suggest the two methods found in the previous chapter: consideration of individual words and phrases as in *lectio divina,* or consideration of the scene in one of the modes of Ignatian mental prayer (meditation or imaginative reconstruction). Let me offer specific examples, using the first Joyful Mystery.

The first Joyful Mystery, as noted, is the Annunciation. The suggested Gospel text for this mystery (event, scene) is Luke 1:26–31, 34–35, 38:

> In the sixth month the angel Gabriel was sent by God to a town in Galilee called Nazareth, to a virgin engaged to a man whose name was Joseph, of the house of David. The virgin's name was Mary. And he came to her and said, "Greetings, favored one! The Lord is with you." But she was much perplexed by his words and pondered what sort of greeting this might be. The angel said to her, "Do not be afraid, Mary, for you have found favor with God. And now, you will conceive in your womb and bear a son, and you will name him Jesus." Mary said to the angel, "How can this be, since I am a virgin?" The angel said to her, "The Holy Spirit will come upon you, and the power of the

Most High will overshadow you; therefore the child to be born will be holy; he will be called Son of God." Then Mary said, "Here am I, the servant of the Lord; let it be with me according to your word." Then the angel departed from her.

First Method of Attention to the Text

The first way we might pay attention to this text in the context of Rosary recitation is simply to listen to the words, and stay with the first word that hooks us. This is highly individual. What strikes you might be different than what strikes me, and what stands out for you on one day may differ from that which stands out on the next day of the particular set of mysteries. This is very similar to the practice of *lectio divina*. What differs is the background of repetitive verbal prayer, and the necessary movement to a different text for the next decade.

Now when I read or listen to the text for the mystery of the Annunciation, I know that on various occasions different words have hooked me. Today, as I write this, it is the word *angel*. Let me present the text again, with *angel* italicized:

In the sixth month the *angel* Gabriel was sent by God to a town in Galilee called Nazareth, to a virgin engaged to a man whose name was Joseph, of the house of David. The virgin's name was Mary. And he came to her and said, "Greetings, favored one! The Lord is with you." But she was much perplexed by his words and pondered what sort of greeting this might be. The *angel* said to her, "Do not be afraid, Mary, for you have found favor with God. And now, you will conceive in your womb and bear a son, and you will name him Jesus." Mary said to the *angel,* "How can this be, since I am a virgin?" The *angel* said to her, "The Holy Spirit will come upon you, and the power of the Most High will overshadow you; therefore the child to be born will be holy; he will be called Son of God." Then Mary said, "Here am I, the servant of the Lord; let it be with me according to your word." Then the *angel* departed from her.

So I'm hooked on the word *angel.* How do I stay with this word? Let me offer an example by presenting what actually happened in my mind and heart, much more rapidly than this account would suggest. My first thoughts were a series of questions: "Now, exactly what is an angel? And do they really appear to people and offer them a choice that will shape the rest of their, and others' lives? And has it happened to me, without me really understanding what it was?" As those thoughts occurred, I recognized that the Church certainly teaches that angels are real, that they are spiritual beings, and that they can and do influence us. The Church even teaches that we each have an individual guardian angel. But are angels real for me? And if they do influence me, am I, or can I become, aware of it?

This led me to a deeper reflection. As noted in the first chapter, from the standpoint of the Church, reality is much more complex than what is available to my physical senses. Science tells me the same thing. I consider my eyes. I learned about light in general science class. Visible light is a very small band on the electromagnetic spectrum. On the lower end of the spectrum are radio waves (radio and TV transmissions), then microwaves (radar and cooking), then infrared light (heat), then visible light, then ultraviolet light (skin cancer), then x-rays, and gamma rays. Now what if I limited my understanding and experience and use of electromagnetic energy to the narrow band visible to my eyes? Wouldn't I be depriving myself of much that is useful and helpful, both physically and intellectually? Wouldn't my world be much smaller and difficult? Using this as an analogy, I come to understand that the Church is simply saying that another spectrum, this time of all living beings, is larger than that which is present to my physical senses or their technological extensions (e.g., telescopes, electron microscopes, and the like). It affirms that there is an entire level of being beyond the scope of my senses, the realm of spiritual beings. And just as science can open me to the possibility of increasingly more numerous dimensions of the empirical world, so can the Church open me to a beyond-the-empirical reality.

But how can I experience something that is not present to my physical senses? Now I believe that the air is filled with electromagnetic waves that I can't physically see because I can turn on a TV or radio and talk on my cell phone. There is tangible proof that I live in a sea of energy that I can't physically see. But what about angels? How can I come to some similar proof of their existence and role in my life?

As I continue to reflect on the word *angel,* and now seek to find some hint or rumor of them in my experience, I recognize logically that I have to begin by choosing to accept the possibility of their existence. Then I recall that it has always been the Church's position that angels communicate primarily by suggestion. An idea pops into my head out of nowhere that my child needs a word of love and affirmation, or that my mother would appreciate a call, or that I should really begin to moderate my eating or time on the phone. Or I'm suddenly inspired to paint a particular scene in a specific way, or hear the words to a song I'm struggling to write, or wake up with an image from a dream that resolves a particular personal or intellectual problem. Now all of these common human experiences can be explained without using angels as the explanation. And we live in an intellectual culture that laughs at such an explanation as childish or superstitious.

But what would happen to me as an adult if I entertain the possibility that angels are real and do seek my well-being? Perhaps it would be similar to what happened to my wife when she began to take lessons in watercolor painting. Suddenly she began to experience a richness and depth to her visual world that was new. Instead of trees and mountains she was seeing textures and tones, and feeling the energy of these creatures in an entirely new and deeply satisfying way. And what she was seeing had always been there. It was not as if there was new information presented to her; she had simply been trained to turn on and tune in to a different channel.

So now I want to try to turn on and tune in to the "angelic channel." I begin with a deep affirmation of the reality of the angelic realm. What I will do after finishing the Rosary is to begin to associate positive thoughts, inspirations, and intuitions as having their origin from within this realm. And then I will consider any unusual coincidences or circumstances that lead to positive outcomes as influenced by angels. And see what happens.

Second Method of Attention to the Text

A second way to pay attention to the texts associated with the individual Rosary mysteries is to attend to the scene as a whole, like one of the forms of Ignatian mental prayer. For this particular text, my personal preference is the Ignatian meditative (analytic) mode. Let's recall the text:

> In the sixth month the angel Gabriel was sent by God to a town in Galilee called Nazareth, to a virgin engaged to a man whose name was Joseph, of the house of David. The virgin's name was Mary. And he came to her and said, "Greetings, favored one! The Lord is with you." But she was much perplexed by his words and pondered what sort of greeting this might

be. The angel said to her, "Do not be afraid, Mary, for you have found favor with God. And now, you will conceive in your womb and bear a son, and you will name him Jesus." Mary said to the angel, "How can this be, since I am a virgin?" The angel said to her, "The Holy Spirit will come upon you, and the power of the Most High will overshadow you; therefore the child to be born will be holy; he will be called Son of God." Then Mary said, "Here am I, the servant of the Lord; let it be with me according to your word." Then the angel departed from her.

When I attend to this text analytically, what strikes me is that this is Mary's moment of vocation—much like Moses at the Burning Bush or Peter or Levi when Jesus first invites them to follow him. This is the moment of decision that will shape her and untold numbers of others' lives. Now we all know the outcome, and all the points along the way. But did Mary? And did she really see the angel Gabriel? And was the decision she made rational? And what about her view of herself as the handmaid of the Lord, servant of this particular work?

I know as I sit with this scene, at age fifty-four, with more than half of my life behind me, a marriage of thirty-one years, two children, a grandson, beginning my twenty-fifth year at the University of Scranton, tenured and fully promoted and department chair, it is easy to see my annunciation moment. It was November 26, 1971, early in the morning. I was a senior theology major at Notre Dame, a conscientious objector to the war in Viet Nam, and had plans to spend at least part of my Christmas break at Our Lady of Mepkin Trappist Monastery in Moncks Corner, South Carolina. I was seriously considering entering the Trappists after graduation, and wanted to get a sense of what it was really like.

Since I'm obviously not a Trappist at Mepkin today, I must have changed my mind in a significant way. So what happened? Well, my senior year I lived off-campus with four friends. A group of St. Mary's College seniors (young women) lived around the corner. As Thanksgiving approached they decided to have a major dinner for off-campus friends who didn't go home for the holidays. I found my name at a seat next to a very attractive young woman from New Jersey, whom I had met once, the previous spring. She had arranged the seating. After a wonderful meal and even more wonderful evening together, I awoke the next morning with a major dilemma. You know the Robert Frost poem, "The Road Not Taken"? It begins:

> Two roads diverged in a yellow wood,
> And sorry I could not travel both
> And be one traveler, long I stood
> And looked down one as far as I could
> To where it bent in the undergrowth;
>
> Then took the other... [5]

On Thursday, November 25, 1971, before dinner, there was one path in front of me. Early Friday morning, November 26, 1971, there were two. Life as a Trappist monk or life "in the world with Marilyn." I sat in a chair in my quiet living room at 810 Napoleon Avenue looking down both paths. And this may sound bizarre, but what I realized was that choosing the Trappists would be a selfish choice, for me. Given my personality, the quiet, the solitude, the beautiful grounds on the Cooper River, the liturgical life, the freedom from a whole host of responsibilities (finding a job, dealing with the Spartanburg, South Carolina, draft board, etc.) was very attractive. Life with Marilyn, on the other hand, contained so many unknowns. And I had a deep intuition that it would challenge me in ways that would never be possible at Mepkin. It would call me out from my deep, but developmentally normal, young adult self-concern.

Now I can't exactly explain how I knew or saw the difference between the two paths. But it was absolutely clear. I didn't see or hear any angels pointing out the right direction, either. But when I consider that our tradition teaches us that angels do exist and can present images to our imaginations, spark our memories, inspire our intellects, warm our hearts, and even influence our external senses and circumstances, I am certainly open to the possibility that my guardian angel was working on me.

The question was, how would I respond to this invitation, making a decision that would obviously shape my adult life? Somehow I simply knew the right choice: life in the world with Marilyn. It was the more challenging, but life-giving path. Then I sat with it for a week, spending every possible moment with Marilyn. Was I ready to jump off the cliff, find a job, marry a Yankee (just kidding)? Well, after a very short time I simply couldn't imagine myself in the future without her. So a week after my annunciation (vocation) moment, I proposed—certainly without fully understanding the joys and sufferings that would lie ahead. That was thirty-two years ago. Since then Marilyn and I have raised two children; nursed four parents and a step-mother through their last days; made and lost friends; paid innumerable bills; cleaned house countless times; been sick, scared, and lonely; and now we are grandparents. And I know for a fact that no monastery could have asked more from me, stretched me more, and encouraged me to be more understanding, compassionate, and forgiving (both of self and others) than the life I have lived since graduation from college.

So when I hear the gospel text for the first Joyful Mystery, I am pulled into intimacy with Mary. I feel her hesitation at the enormity of the decision, her concern with God's obvious confidence in her, and her ultimate giving over of self-will to ongoing responsiveness to God. And I am reminded of a passage in Walter Ciszek's *He Leadeth Me*:

> It is in choosing to serve God, to do his will, that man achieves his highest and fullest freedom. It may sound paradoxical to say that our highest and fullest freedom comes when we follow to the least detail the will of another, but it is true nonethe-

less when that other is God....I realized then, and I felt it more deeply each day, that true freedom meant nothing else than letting God operate within my soul without interference, giving preference to God's will as manifested in the promptings, inspirations, and other means he chose to communicate, rather than acting on my own initiatives.[6]

And I sit with this, while my ten Hail Marys seem to say themselves in the background. If I happen to be praying the Rosary alone, and this particular mystery is very powerful for me, it's perfectly fine to stay with it for the next four decades. Or if the second or third mystery really speaks to me, I may stay with those for the remainder of the Rosary. Obviously if I'm praying with others, I will move through the mysteries with the group.

What this third level of practice does is ground me deeply in what our two-thousand-year-old tradition has come to hold as the most significant moments in the story of our salvation. And as I become more and more familiar with these twenty mysteries, I become more and more conformed to Christ, with Mary as my guide. I see Jesus through her eyes, from conception to ascension. His story becomes more and more my story. These twenty mysteries become the framework of meaning, the interpretive filter, for my own life.

When this begins to happen, the result is often the gift *(tariki)* of a deeper level of knowing. This is made possible by the *jiriki* of saying the Rosary on a regular basis, by really beginning to sit with the scenes from Jesus' life. This is making myself available, serving the work. What we are doing, in a very real way, is being disciples. We are following Jesus, as did those who originally joined him. We are walking with Jesus, from conception to ascension. And as we walk, we deepen our understanding and appreciation of who he is and what he has and continues to do for us. And sometimes that understanding reaches a depth that is beyond words. Let me offer an illustration.

Earlier in the chapter I offered my own sitting with the first Joyful Mystery, and spoke about my own annunciation moment. In my own practice, as I became accustomed to the entire cycle of mysteries, I began to see connections that weren't apparent initially. For example, in the account of the Annunciation, the angel Gabriel says that Mary will conceive, will have God incarnate come to life within her, by the "overshadowing" of the Holy Spirit. Now overshadowing is a very unusual word, and I see it only one other time in the Rosary Mysteries—the Transfiguration. The Transfiguration is the fourth Luminous Mystery, and the suggested reading is Luke 9:28–36:

> Now about eight days after these sayings Jesus took with him Peter and John and James, and went up on the mountain to pray. And while he was praying, the appearance of his face changed, and his clothes became dazzling white. Suddenly

they saw two men, Moses and Elijah, talking to him. They appeared in glory and were speaking of his departure, which he was about to accomplish at Jerusalem. Now Peter and his companions were weighed down with sleep; but since they had stayed awake, they saw his glory and the two men who stood with him. Just as they were leaving him, Peter said to Jesus, "Master, it is good for us to be here; let us make three dwellings, one for you, one for Moses, and one for Elijah"—not knowing what he said. While he was saying this, a cloud came and *overshadowed* them; and they were terrified as they entered the cloud. Then from the cloud came a voice that said, "This is my Son, my Chosen; listen to him!" When the voice had spoken, Jesus was found alone. And they kept silent and in those days told no one any of the things they had seen.

This account tells of the first time that the inner circle of the disciples really saw the divinity of Jesus, although they certainly knew there was something very different and special about their Master. When we see them at the beginning of the account of the Transfiguration, they seem astonished and confused by what is happening. Then they are "overshadowed" by the cloud, and gain clarity. Now for me, the overshadowing has a connection to the

Annunciation. The disciples' realization of Jesus' divinity came to life in them in the same manner that the Son of God came to life in Mary's womb—by God's grace, the *overshadowing*. Perhaps their deep realization could be termed a *transfiguration moment*. This was the point in their journey with Jesus when they had a particularly deep realization of his true nature. And I know that I have had similar transfiguration moments as I have followed Jesus with the Rosary. And it is just such *tariki* moments that have helped me appreciate how intimately we can come to know and feel Jesus' presence within our hearts and minds. This is exactly what Pope John Paul II seeks to convey in his own meditation on this fourth Luminous Mystery:

> The Gospel scene of Christ's transfiguration, in which the three Apostles Peter, James, and John appear entranced by the beauty of the Redeemer, can be seen as *an icon of Christian contemplation*. To look upon the face of Christ, to recognize its mystery amid the daily events and the sufferings of his human life, and then to grasp the divine splendor definitively revealed in the Risen Lord, seated in glory at the right hand of the Father: this is the task of every follower of Christ and therefore the task of each one of us. In contemplating Christ's face we become open to receiving the mystery of Trinitarian life, experiencing ever anew

the love of the Father and delighting in
the joy of the Holy Spirit. Saint Paul's
words can then be applied to us:
"Beholding the glory of the Lord, we are
being changed into his likeness, from one
degree of glory to another" (2 Cor 3:18).[7]

So what begins simply as repetitive verbal prayer *(jiriki)* can
develop into a deeply contemplative (in the non-Ignatian
sense, the *tariki* sense) practice. The Rosary can become a
grace-filled gateway into a deeply felt and experienced intimacy with the Son of God, an intimacy that is so power-
fully transformative that in the words of the second letter
of Peter, we may "become participants of the divine
nature" (2 Pet 1:4).

Let me conclude this chapter with a more concrete
image. The word *Rosary* is derived from the Latin
Rosarium, literally a rose garden. In his very engaging, *The
Treasures of God*, Fr. Raymond Gunzel offers a beautiful
way of viewing the Rosary:

> The rosary itself is a closed circle of beads,
> offering an image of a garden. Tradi-
> tionally, a garden was a walled, protected,
> and safe place cut off from the dangers
> and distractions of the outside world. It
> was a refuge wherein the soul and body
> could find a safe harbor in which to heal
> and nourish the soul. The rosary is a

prayer sanctuary in which our mind and spirit can find refuge.[8]

To put this into the language I have been using, saying the Rosary can become a sacred space for us, a garden we can enter to see the light and hear angels speak. Each day we can enter this garden of roses, leaving cares and concerns behind for a while, and spend time with the Lord. And, to give new meaning to an old cliché, take time to "smell the roses."

CHAPTER THREE
Exercise 1

I want you to do an Ignatian contemplation. But instead of a gospel text as a subject, I want you to imagine that you are watching a short film entitled: *The Story of My Life.* What would you see and hear? Now don't think about it, just let the little film play on the Technicolor screen of your imagination. Do it now. What do you see, hear, feel, taste, touch, and smell as you view the images of your life from earliest memories to most cherished future hopes, dreams, and aspirations? What are those dreams? Now when the film ends, jot down answers to the following questions, without thinking too long, hard, or deeply about your responses, and based on what you have just "viewed."

- What is the beginning of the story?
- What are the Joyful, Luminous, Sorrowful, and Glorious Mysteries of your life thus far?
- Presuming you are the main character, who is the supporting cast?
- For the main character (you), briefly:

  * Describe your personality.
  * List your hopes and dreams.
  * List your fears.
  * Describe your view of human nature (good, bad, mixed; possessing free will or not; and the role of heredity/genetics and culture in personal development).
  * Indicate the primary means you use to achieve your hopes and dreams (e.g., hard work, money, education, connections, parents, friends, God, and of course, the lottery).

- Answer the question, "Life is a _____?"
- What is the main theme of my story?

Now, when you are done, put it away. Forget about it for a day or a week. That's it. Don't read further. Continue whatever spiritual practice you are currently using, get some physical exercise, enjoy nature, socialize, be human. And then when you've forgotten about what you've written in this exercise, when you can come back to it with fresh eyes, open to the next chapter.

CHAPTER FOUR
Exercise 2

*N*ow what I want you to do is to look at the previous exercise as if a stranger wrote it. What can you tell me about the person who wrote it, based only on what's written? Tell me everything, in a page. Can you determine gender, age, culture, education? Emotional makeup, personality, character? Attitude to life, philosophy of life, basic assumptions? And what about the hopes, fears, power to attain dreams. And how do you feel or what do you think about the "Life is" and "theme" responses? What is the underlying story of this person's life? Take some time to do this reflection before you move to chapter five.

CHAPTER FIVE
The Mass

*T*he purpose of the two preceding practical exercises was to make you receptive to the idea that we unconsciously see our own lives as a narrative, a story with ourselves as the main character. Why is that?

Well, let's think about it. How did we develop our sense of identity, our idea of who "me" is? Through relationships, I think. Through the feedback we get from others, and especially from the feedback we received in our first years of life (the most important of which is likely beyond recall). And we are at the center. In our development we were rewarded or punished for certain behaviors, and likely modified our behavior to gain reward and avoid punishment. And through this process we learned that we were smart or athletic or artistic or physically attractive or stupid, clumsy, sloppy, or ugly or—more likely—some unique combination of these and other characteristics of self (angry/calm, happy/sad, etc.).

So from the beginning we received information from our human environment that we used to form our sense of self. And simultaneously we received a picture of life, what the world is all about, what's most important and how to gain it, a world view. It is a story that tells us what it is to be a male or female, white or black or brown or yellow or red, an American or Canadian or Mexican, a southerner or Yankee, Catholic or Baptist or Jewish. And above all it gives us a plot for life, with an ultimate goal or destination or reward.

One standard American plot (story, worldview) is: "If you just work hard, you will succeed." Success is the ultimate goal (destination, reward), and is understood to be wealth, fame, or power. It's uncanny (my guardian angel?), but as I compose this I hear Randy Newman's "It's Money That Matters in the USA" playing in the background on the Web radio station I'm tuned to.

I think if we're honest, and I certainly include myself here, down deep this is our deepest conviction. Don't most of us really believe that if we just had X amount of money, we'd be safe, happy, secure, and completely satisfied? And doesn't this deep, almost unconscious belief structure most of our life? Isn't most of our time and energy focused on money? Managing what we have and trying to get more, or worrying about bills and college education and retirement, or looking for the newest or best products, or shopping? The difficulty is that working hard doesn't always lead to success. The plot seems to be faulty, at least for a significant number of Americans (not to mention the rest of the world).

Now along with this American success story line, there is another competing story in my life. To the extent that I see myself as a child, a sibling, a friend, a lover, a spouse, a parent, there is the story of relationships. I look back over my life and see the significant people and how they have shaped me and become part of who I am. And what drives me in these relationships is the same as what drives me to seek the salvation of the American Dream—the goals of safety, happiness, security, and satisfaction. But here these goals are understood to be attained through working hard at human relationships rather than material acquisition.

Now for me, there is a third story. It is found in a very compressed form in the Catholic Mass. Let me offer the brief version found in one of the basic Eucharistic Prayers, the section of the Mass just before the bread and wine are consecrated:

> Father, we acknowledge your greatness: all your actions show your wisdom and love. You formed man in your own likeness and set him over the whole world to serve you, his creator, and to rule over all creatures. Even when he disobeyed you and lost your friendship you did not abandon

him to the power of death, but helped
men to seek and find you. Again and
again you offered a covenant to man, and
through the prophets taught him to hope
for salvation. Father, you so loved the
world that in the fullness of time you sent
your only Son to be our Savior. He was
conceived through the power of the Holy
Spirit, and born of the Virgin Mary, a
man like us in all things but sin. To the
poor he proclaimed the good news of salvation, to prisoners freedom, and to those
in sorrow, joy. In fulfillment of your will
he gave himself up to death; but by rising
from the dead, he destroyed death and
restored life. And that we may no longer
live for ourselves but for him, he sent the
Holy Spirit from you, Father, as his first
gift to those who believe, to complete his
work on earth and bring us the fullness of
grace.[1]

Now let me offer an alternative version, given by
Buddhist scholar David Loy. In writing about the two most
significant stories in his life, those of the Buddha and Jesus,
he understands the story of Jesus, the Christian plot as:

The source of the cosmos becoming
embodied in a human being, who loves
all of us so much that he is willing to die

for us; who empties himself completely in order to become a vehicle for the cosmic process, in the process modeling what each of us needs to do in our own lives; who has no need for money or fame or temporal power, but urges us to see through them as traps that only interfere with our higher spiritual destiny; who, most fundamentally, taught that the highest meaning of life is to love—not merely those who love us, but everyone, especially those who need our love the most, those in greatest need.[2]

I think Loy understands the story perfectly. Together these two concise accounts describe the outline of my third story. Now, because I learned this third story as a child from my parents and in the Church, and because of the sort of child I was, this story became the basic plot of my life. I was a child who could gaze for hours at clouds, seeing a parade of strange and magical shapes. I was a child who read Greek mythology as avidly as the comic books that filled my room. I was a child who loved the secret places and intricate ceremonies and constantly evolving games of childhood. To play was to be alive.

This child, who still is alive within me, loved the liturgical life of the pre-Vatican II Catholic Church: a strange, mysterious language, bells, incense, candles, Benediction, vestments, sacraments, processions, chants— and this had the effect of rooting the Christian story deeply into my heart and imagination. I think what happened was that this rich experience gave me a taste of something I wanted more of, a certain presence that beckoned me. And it haunts me to this day, a need, a hunger, to taste God, to enter the presence of the Holy. And I felt it very intensely, as I think back, during Holy Week.

I remember Easter week especially because my family would spend it in Charleston, South Carolina, usually on the Isle of Palms. It was too cold to swim, but my three younger brothers and I would forget time, walking the shore or playing in the dunes. Each day my parents would take us to a different church to celebrate what were to me the central events of the most important story of my life. And Easter Sunday morning was the culmination. It helped that Charleston would be bursting with color—azaleas, camellias, wisteria; the smell of narcissus and lilies; and the Easter finery of folks both white and black. Life was especially rich and un-ordinary on this day. And I still hear the cathedral's youth choir singing "Christ the Lord is ris'n today." Holy Week Masses were sacred times and those churches were sacred places. And I was blessed to have these deeply formative experiences, and to be gently taught to see them as moments of intimacy with God, communion.

I do know that my present understanding and appreciation of Mass and the story it enacts is based on these early experiences wherein communion with God was connected to liturgy and church, sacred rite and sacred place. Today such a connection is less common. Nonetheless, everyone has experienced intimacy with God, glimpses of glory. It's just that it's not so often connected with Mass and the church building, and in many cases is not recognized for what it is.

Beginning with those Holy Weeks, now fifty years ago, I have come to recognize this Presence as an ever-faithful source of consolation and inspiration. Often I have felt it in beautiful natural settings, or as the recipient of the spontaneous love and goodness of those special people in my life. But even more often I have been touched by this loving Source in places hallowed by the prayers of good people, like the Grotto at the University of Notre Dame or Stella Maris Church on Sullivan's Island, South Carolina, or a little Shinto shrine hidden in the woods on a cliff overlooking the ocean on the Izu peninsula in Japan. And I feel it almost physically whenever I enter a Catholic church.

Now why do I feel this so strongly in a Catholic church? Why is any Catholic church a sacred place for me? The answer is not complicated. I was taught the doctrine of the Real Presence as a child, taught that Jesus was objectively present in the consecrated bread reserved in the tabernacle. And as a child, I simply took it to be the case. Now obviously as a middle-aged grandfather, having passed through typically human cognitive development, this belief has been tested. But this testing has led to an even deeper appreciation and acceptance of the Real Presence, so much so that whenever I enter a Catholic church, I immediately enter sacred space. I leave a world centered on my needs and concerns, and open myself to the One who the story of my faith teaches me is my Creator, the Source of all that is good and true and beautiful. God becomes the Center, and I sit in that Presence.

Sitting in a Catholic church in this fashion is usually referred to as *eucharistic adoration.* As a spiritual practice it is wonderful. But it is still an individual devotion. Much deeper and more powerful is the communal celebration of the Eucharist, the Mass, because it is a deep hearing of and participation in what I referred to earlier as my third story, a highly compressed retelling of one of the most significant stories of humankind. This is the story I learned as a child, from parents and church, and "played in" during Holy Week in Charleston. Parents, and church especially in the Mass, told me that empirical reality was created by an all-powerful and all-loving God for the mutual benefit of all creatures. Of course I was told this in language appropriate for my age. I was also told that above or beyond or within this created world was a more profound reality that sustained me and that would ultimately lead me to a joy that surpassed any Christmas gift—past, present, and to come. And I also learned that I could have an incredibly intimate experience of this all-loving God when I came of age and could physically take God into myself under the appearance of bread and wine. So Mass became a gateway for me, a rite (set pattern of words, symbols, and actions) that offered me a foretaste of the ultimate goal, heaven. It was a ceremonial retelling that put me into the story in a very powerful way.

So what is it like to participate in Mass in this way? Perhaps I could take you with me to Mass. For our visit, I would choose a daily Mass. They are usually celebrated three times a day: early morning, noon, and late afternoon. Attendance is typically light, especially in the morning. There is time for coming to quiet before Mass begins, and freedom to remain when Mass concludes. And there is a very subtle energy present, likely the result of the devotion and holiness of those present.

We arrive ten or fifteen minutes early. Before entering the church proper, we dip our right fingers into a receptacle (small or large), containing holy water, and make the sign of the cross. Let me explain both.

The sign of the cross is the practice of touching the right hand to one's forehead, then chest, then left shoulder, and right shoulder while saying vocally or sub-vocally: "In the name of the Father, and of the Son, and of the Holy Spirit, Amen." As Father Joseph Champlin explains:

> The words and gesture that form the sign of the cross express our major Christian mysteries. We believe in one God (in the "name" not "names") and three Persons—Father, Son, and Holy Spirit. The cross itself recalls Calvary, the crucifixion, the dying of Jesus for us. But before Christ could do this on our behalf, he first had to enter our world through the birth at Christmas. And we never stop at Good Friday, but move on through Holy Saturday to Easter and the Resurrection. Consequently, and usually unconsciously,

> we manifest through the spoken and
> acted out sign of the cross faith in the
> oneness of God, the Trinity, the
> Incarnation, and Redemption.[3]

Holy water is water blessed by a priest. To use it in conjunction with the sign of the cross as we enter church adds a reminder of our own baptism into the faith signified by the sign of the cross. It is also a symbolic act of cleansing and purification, and a bodily means of reminding ourselves that we are entering sacred space.

When we enter the church, we move to a pew and genuflect before entering. Genuflection is a Western form of reverence that Catholics use to show deep respect for the Real Presence in the tabernacle. Once we have entered the pew, we take a few moments, sitting or kneeling, to come to quiet and remember where we are. This is a holy place because the consecrated bread is reserved in the tabernacle. The sanctuary lamp, a candle suspended from the ceiling usually in a red glass globe or cylinder, reminds us of this. It reminds us, in the words of Cardinal Joseph Ratzinger, that: "The Lord has definitively drawn this piece of matter to himself....The Lord himself is present. The whole Christ is there."[4] We bring ourselves to a felt experience of the holiness of this place, and our typically hurried, list-oriented sense of "not enough time in the day" falls away. We move out of being obsessed with what happened yesterday, or what will happen tomorrow, and move into the now. We become present to the present moment. We re-collect our scatteredness, and move out of a chronological sense of time passing. We simply are where we are, right now. And a sense of depth opens up. This is sacred time. It is wonderful that we can bring ourselves to this experience before Mass begins.

The Mass Itself

Introductory Rite

At daily Mass, the priest enters wearing ceremonial garments called vestments. Their main symbolic function is to "make clear that he (the priest) is not there as a private person, as this or that man, but stands in the place of Another—Christ. What is merely private, merely individual, about him should disappear and make way for Christ...Vestments are a reminder of this, of this transformation in Christ..."[5]

The first thing the priest does is kiss the altar. Traditionally the altar symbolizes Christ, and since the Middle Ages has a space for a hollowed out stone containing relics of saints. Thus kissing the altar "is a special and solemn gesture of reverence for Christ, for his special followers enshrined in the altar, and for this holy place at which the sacred mysteries will soon be celebrated."[6] The priest then moves to the presider's chair, and together with the congregation, makes the sign of the cross, which has already been explained. He then formally greets the congregation and may make comments about the scriptural readings or themes of this particular celebration. His greeting to us as a group transforms us from a collection of individuals pursuing private devotion into a community of prayer, gathered for the same purpose.

We then move to a moment of silence and are asked to call to mind our sinfulness and to express our sorrow and desire for change. This is very significant, but requires a clear understanding of what sin is. Perhaps many of us understand sin as something bad we've done, said, or thought. Well, actually those bad thoughts, words, and deeds are the effects of sin, rather than sin itself. The root sense of the word *sin*, in the Bible, is drawn from the language of warfare. It means to "miss the mark," in the sense of missing a target, a bull's eye. To recognize my sinfulness is to see where I have missed the target with family, friends, professional responsibilities. It doesn't mean I have to see myself as an evil person, but simply as someone trying hard but at times falling short. The reason that such a recognition is important at this point in the Mass is that we are being led to our first experience of the Lord (in scripture), and he has told us that, "Those who are well have no need of a physician, but those who are sick; I have come to call not the righteous but sinners" (Mark 2:17). Think about it: We don't go to a doctor until we say to ourselves, "I'm sick." To go to meet the Physician, don't we have to recognize our need for healing? The priest then concludes this penitential rite most appropriately, with the prayer: "May almighty God have mercy on us, forgive us our sins, and bring us to everlasting life. Amen." Then, depending on the day and season, the Gloria may be said. The Introductory Rites conclude with a final prayer, after which we sit.

Liturgy of the Word

This first major portion of the Mass centers on readings from Old and New Testaments. What we seek here is Christ's presence as word in the scriptural texts, as we will seek it later in the consecrated bread and wine. This experience of the word should be familiar from chapter one and the practice of *lectio divina*. In fact, if we use the daily readings as the subject for a *lectio* or Ignatian mental prayer (either style) before Mass, the Liturgy of the Word will become a very powerful experience of intimacy with God as word.

At daily Mass there is typically a first reading from the Old or New Testament. There should then be a period of silence, followed by a responsorial psalm and another brief moment of silence. Following the psalm, the priest prays quietly asking a blessing on his reading of the Gospel, and the congregation rises and communally recites or sings the Alleluia. The priest (or deacon) then announces the gospel text to be read, and all make the sign of the cross on the forehead, lips, and heart. "This gesture, often curiously made and frequently not understood, denotes our desire to grasp the words of Christ with our minds, speak them with our lips, and believe them with our hearts."[7] The Gospel is then read, and there may or may not be a homily (instructive commentary on one or more of the readings, with a practical application).

On weekdays we move from the homily immediately to a series of general intercessory prayers (prayers of supplication), omitting the Credo. This may be followed by the opportunity to offer individual petitions. This concludes the Liturgy of the Word, and we now move to the second major portion of the Mass, the Liturgy of the Eucharist.

Liturgy of the Eucharist

At the conclusion of the intercessions the congregation sits as the priest moves to the altar and prepares it. The bread is elevated as the priest "blesses" God through whose "goodness we have this bread to offer, which earth has given and human hands have made. It will become for us the bread of life." This prayer turns our attention to God, and God's gifts of food, human talents, and the coming transformation of the bread into the body of Christ. Then the priest pours wine into the chalice, with several drops of water, while quietly saying: "By the mystery of this water and wine may we come to share in the divinity of Christ, who humbled himself to share in our humanity." This is a complex symbol, representing at least the following six different things:

> ...the union of divine and human elements in Christ; the descent of God's Son into this world becoming one of us; the close bond between Christ and his Church; the elevation of Christians, through baptism, to a sharing by grace of Jesus' divine nature; the pouring out of blood and water from the Savior's side on the cross; and the intimate union of Christ and ourselves...."[8]

That's quite a bit of meaning packed into a single, simple action. And if we are aware of this many-layered symbolism, we have the possibility of a very deep moment of reflection on our ultimate destiny, and the role Jesus has in it. Through his sacrifice we have the opportunity of entering into the deepest possible intimacy with God, and all those united with God.

Returning to the order of the liturgy, the priest now blesses the wine with the same words used over the bread. He then inaudibly says, "Lord God, we ask you to receive us and be pleased with the sacrifice we offer you with humble and contrite hearts." He then washes his hands, quietly saying "Lord, wash away my iniquity; cleanse me from my sin." Then moving to the center of the altar with hands extended over the bread and wine, he invites the congregation to: "Pray, brethren, that our sacrifice may be acceptable to God, the almighty Father." The congregation replies: "May the Lord accept the sacrifice at your hands, for the praise and glory of his name, for our good, and the good of all his Church." Thus we, people and priest, pray to God to send his Spirit to change the bread and wine into the body and blood of Christ. At this point the preparation of the gifts is complete, and we move to the climax of the liturgy, the Eucharistic Prayer.

Eucharist is derived from the Greek, and means "thanksgiving" or "to give thanks." This section of the Mass is called the Eucharistic Prayer because thanksgiving is a central theme. Its beginning, called the Preface, starts appropriately with the priest's request of the congregation to "give thanks to the Lord our God," and their reply: "It is right to give him thanks and praise." The priest then addresses a prayer to the Father, saying that "we do well always and everywhere to give you thanks," and concludes it with the affirmation that "with all the choirs of angels in heaven we proclaim your glory and join in their unending hymn of praise: Holy, holy, holy...."

What this concluding section of the Preface presumes is that there is an ongoing, eternal liturgy in heaven, and that at this moment we are invited to join it. This is a deep mystery. Let me attempt an explanation. There is a type of joy in life that has to be shared to be complete. When my son Jon and daughter Anna were born, both times I *had* to call both sets of parents, siblings, best friends, and colleagues to share the good news. I was so full of joy I thought I would burst. Catholics believe such a joy is at the heart of creation. The created world is the outflowing of God's essential joy. There is a beautiful image of this living, flowing, divine joy in the book of Revelation, "the river of the water of life, bright as crystal, flowing from the throne of God and of the Lamb" (Rev 22:1). Jean Corbon uses this image to explain the significance of Jesus' death and resurrection and the nature of the heavenly liturgy:

> ...when the incarnation occurred, the river entered our world and assumed our flesh. In the "hour" of the cross and resurrection it sprang forth from the incorruptible and life-giving body of Christ.[9]

Then when Christ ascended to the Father, the "river" returned to its Source. And it is this movement of joyful return to the Father that is the essence of the heavenly liturgy. In heaven, all are immersed in the current of this living joy, which is the essence of God. This is what heaven is, this is what our ultimate destination and complete fulfillment is, the ever-deepening experience of the flow of joy. And this flow is what is meant by the heavenly liturgy. And from the standpoint of the Church, we actually entered this river of living joy at baptism.

Now I didn't say we felt this, experienced it, at baptism. But I know I had a moment of it that spring morning forty years ago. I was gently enfolded and immersed in the river of God. So to get to the bottom line, what the concept of heavenly liturgy tries to express is that this river is always flowing, and we are invited to really feel our immersion in it at Mass. The invitation may slip past us, though. It occurs when the priest invites us to proclaim, "together with all the angels and saints," the "Holy, Holy, Holy," also called the *Sanctus*.

This proclamation is taken almost directly from the book of the prophet Isaiah. The scene is the moment when Isaiah receives his vocation in a vision of God in heaven. It reads:

> In the year that King Uzziah died, I saw the Lord sitting on a throne, high and lofty; and the hem of his robe filled the temple. Seraphs were in attendance above him; each had six wings: with two they

covered their faces, and with two they covered their feet, and with two they flew. And one called to another and said: "Holy, holy, holy is the Lord of hosts; the whole earth is full of his glory." (Isa 6:1–3)

So when we are asked to praise God with the "Holy, Holy, Holy," "together with all the angels and saints," we are being reminded of this ongoing heavenly praise of God, the eternal liturgy of heaven, and asked to join it. We are being invited:

...through the "door open in heaven" (Rev 4:1) into the joy of the Father! For the liturgy is the celebration of the Father's joy....The heavenly liturgy celebrates the ongoing event of the return of the Son— and of all others in him—to the Father's house.[10]

To return from this brief explanatory digression to the order of the Mass, following the "Holy, Holy, Holy" the priest then proceeds to one of the versions of the Eucharistic Prayer, which has its climax in the consecration of the bread and wine. As a child I was taught that this was the most sacred part of the Mass, and even today I automatically move into deep reverent attention as the priest pronounces "This is my body; this is my blood." And this moment in the Mass:

...when the Lord comes down and transforms bread and wine to become his Body and Blood cannot fail to stun, to the very core of their being, those who participate in the Eucharist by faith and prayer....For a moment the world is silent, everything is silent, and in that silence we touch the eternal—for one beat of the heart we step out of time into God's being-with-us.[11]

Following the words of the consecration, we step back into human time. We pray with the priest for all who have died, and then together recite the Lord's Prayer. We then reach out to one another with some sign of peace, which reminds us that "we must be one with each other in our hearts before daring to become one with each other through receiving the same body and blood of Christ."[12] We then ask the Lamb of God for peace and mercy as the bread is broken and wine poured for distribution. The priest then genuflects and holds the consecrated host before us saying "This is the Lamb of God who takes away the sins of the world. Happy are those who are called to his supper." This reference to the "supper" of the Lamb recalls a beautiful image of heaven found in the book of Revelation: "Blessed are those who are invited to the marriage supper of the Lamb" (Rev 19:9). So we can add this image to that of the river of life as a hint, a suggestion, of the ultimate happiness (what is more wonderful than a wedding reception?) that awaits us. But don't forget, this is also a happiness that we can taste here, now, in this sacred time and place.

Following this invitation to receive the Body and Blood of Christ, we reply in the words of the centurion in Matthew's Gospel: "Lord, I am not worthy to receive you, but only say the word and I shall be healed." As Father Joseph Champlin points out, "His (the centurion's) faith, humility, and confidence are a model for all those baptized waiting to come forward to receive their Lord and Lamb in Communion."[13] This helps us realize how privileged we are to receive into our selves the living Christ under the appearances of bread and wine. This is Holy Communion, our communion with the Holy, with God. This is an opportunity for intimacy with the Lord that goes beyond words and concepts. It is also a very deep communion with all those also consuming the Body and Blood of Christ. "Eating it...is a spiritual process. 'Eating' it means worshipping it. Eating it means letting it come into me, so that my 'I' is transformed and opens up into the great 'we,' so that we become 'one' in him."[14] So as I consume and adore the Lord and enter into very deep intimacy with him, I am simultaneously united (communion) with all those united to him. I am connected both to God and others in a very profound way, a connection that is a real foretaste and prefiguring of heaven, what the Catholic tradition refers to as the *communion of saints*. And I surrender to "the transforming power of God, who wants, through what happens in the liturgy, to transform us and the world"[15] into the kingdom of God.

We then return to our pew for a period of silent worship. There is then a brief prayer, a blessing by the priest, and we are formally dismissed with the words "Go in peace, to love and serve the Lord," to which is often added, "and one another." Thus, when the liturgy is concluded, we are sent out to bring this transformative experience into our daily life and to all those we meet this day. We are encouraged to take all the gifts we have received, and especially the living Lord, and offer them and him, through our words and deeds, to those most in need.

So this is my experience at Mass. During it I enter deeply into my third story, so deeply in fact that it becomes the primary plot of my life. And I have a glimmering of what Paul meant when he said "it is no longer I who live, but it is Christ who lives in me" (Gal 2:20). And this happens because the Mass allows me to move into sacred place and time, experience my human limits, taste God's unconditional love for me (which is at the same time the experience of being forgiven), and enter into an ever-deepening communion with God and "all the saints" that promises complete satisfaction and fulfillment. I swim in the river of divine joy. And I am called to carry this into my daily life, to be the eyes and ears and arms and heart and mind of Christ in the world today. The next chapter will offer some of the traditional ways that this "being Christ for others" can be accomplished, how my Eucharistic communion *(tariki)* can be carried into the world of my daily life.

CHAPTER SIX
Works of Mercy

*T*here is a simple, but profound pattern to Catholic spirituality. I work, I receive God's gift, and then I bring what I have received into my daily life. This creates an ever-deepening movement of growth, both personal and communal, as I return each day to my spiritual practice: jiriki, tariki, incarnation; deeper jiriki, deeper tariki, deeper incarnation. And I like Madeleine L'Engle's term serving the work *as a name for this process.*

What I turn to specifically in this chapter is the *incarnational* moment in this evolutionary process. When Jesus was asked to sum up the path to salvation, he said it was to love God with our entire mind, heart, and strength, and to love our neighbor as our self. This is what we can do, the *jiriki*. In what I have presented thus far, the real focus has been on the *jiriki* of *loving God*: spiritual reading, *lectio divina*, Ignatian mental prayer, the Rosary, and eucharistic liturgy. I have certainly also spoken about the *tariki* or grace that may follow our work, and that it is meant to be shared. But I haven't offered suggestions for this sharing, the *jiriki* of *loving neighbor*. The Catholic spiritual tradition is very helpful in this regard. But before I turn to it, an initial consideration is necessary.

The first step in bringing the fruit of our personal and communal devotion to others, the *jiriki* of loving neighbor, is to be clear about the primary challenge. Just go look at your calendar. If it's like ours, and we are "empty-nesters," it's hard to see the date for all the "things to do" and "people to meet" written in various colors of pen and pencil. Our lives are filled with busyness. There is never enough time in the day to get everything done, and we get out of breath just thinking about it. So to begin to *incarnate* the gifts we have received in private spiritual practice and communal worship, it's necessary to accept the busyness and think about how we actually get things done. For example, if we need to lose weight, we pay attention to our diet, counting Weight Watcher points or eliminating carbs, and become increasingly conscious of what we eat. What asceticism! If we need to reduce debt, we create a budget and record every penny we spend. More self-discipline. So if we want to incorporate the graces we have received in private and communal prayer into our daily lives, we can use the same disciplined approach. Make a list of ways to love neighbor in our daily life, and keep track. And a good set of guidelines to work with is the traditional Catholic corporal and spiritual works of mercy.

Corporal Works of Mercy

The corporal works of mercy are:

1. Feed the hungry.
2. Give drink to the thirsty.
3. Clothe the naked.
4. Offer hospitality to the homeless.
5. Care for the sick.
6. Visit the imprisoned.
7. Bury the dead.

These seven injunctions are derived from the Last Judgment passage in the Gospel of Matthew (25:31–46). They were and continue to be understood literally. The focus is on meeting the immediate physical needs of others (*corporal* = of or belonging to the *body*). At this level their meaning and application is straightforward. We are each called to respond to the immediate physical needs of others. The letter of James (2:13–17) puts this imperative most clearly:

> What good is it, my brothers and sisters, if you say you have faith but do not have works? Can faith save you? If a brother or sister is naked and lacks daily food, and one of you says to them, "Go in peace; keep warm and eat your fill," and yet you

do not supply their bodily needs, what is
the good of that? So faith by itself, if it has
no works, is dead.

So we are called to incarnate our faith, what we have
received in prayer, by meeting the immediate physical
needs of others. For example, we can feed the hungry by
giving time to a local soup kitchen, by donations to a local
food drive, or by preparing meals for a new mother, our
spouse, or our children. And we can give drink to the
thirsty, clothe the naked, shelter the homeless, and care for
the sick in much the same way. But there is an even
broader application, as pointed out by Mitch Finley in his
The Corporal & Spiritual Works of Mercy:

> One can feed the hungry...not only by
> actually providing the necessities of life
> but also by working to correct economic
> abuses which cause unnecessary unem-
> ployment and poverty.[1]

This has obvious application to all the corporal
works of mercy. Many of us have the training and experience to understand and correct the causes of poverty and
its symptoms (insufficient food, shelter, clothing, and med-
ical resources; disease; and crime). And even more of us
have the sensitivity and concern to apply time and material
assets to the promotion of economic and social justice.
When we give of self, time, or money, to such causes, we

should consciously see these as acts of "neighbor-love," as corporal works of mercy.

When one or more of the corporal (and spiritual, as we shall see) works are practiced consistently over a period of time, what begins to happen is that our life begins to take on the shape of Christ's life. We begin to identify more and more with those we love through deeds done on their behalf, and allow God's love to pass through us to them. We become Christ to them. What also typically happens is that we begin to see ourselves and our daily lives in a different way. We see ourselves more and more as disciples of Christ, as servants of the work, and even the smallest and most insignificant acts of our daily lives as part of a ministry of love. The effect of this on our daily spiritual practice, especially on the *tariki* dimension, can be remarkable. Lights and consolations increase.

Spiritual Works of Mercy

The spiritual works of mercy are:

1. Admonish the sinner.
2. Instruct the ignorant.
3. Counsel the doubtful.
4. Comfort the sorrowful.
5. Bear wrongs patiently.
6. Forgive all injuries.
7. Pray for the living and the dead.

While the exact source of this list is difficult to determine, it is found in St. Thomas Aquinas' *Summa Theologica*

(II.II.Q32.Art 2), which was completed toward the end of the thirteenth century. These seven injunctions concern the emotional, psychological, and spiritual needs of others, as well as our relationships to those in our lives who present challenges to our willingness to love. Because they originated in a culture so very different from our own, and deal with more complex issues than the corporal works, commentary on each spiritual work of mercy is necessary.

1. Admonish the Sinner

The online thesaurus I use has the following synonyms for *admonish*: reprove, caution, warn, reprimand, rebuke, reproach, tell off, scold. Now I don't know about you, but if someone admonished me, I would get angry or shut down. And I don't think that's the objective. If this is a way of loving someone, then what I'm trying to do is offer constructive criticism to someone I care about. And this is very difficult to accomplish, because it requires the one who receives the admonishment to be able to really hear what's being said, and the admonisher to be deeply aware of their own frailty.

Perhaps a personal example would be helpful. Thirty-five years ago I was a sophomore in college, spending that year at Sophia University in Tokyo. I lived in a dormitory with other foreign students. The Americans came to know each other well. Before Christmas we were functionally brothers and sisters. At that time in my life I was a real cynic, always tearing down, putting down, being down. At one point in late autumn one of my American "sisters," Carm, had finally had it with my negativity. After one of my unconsciously sarcastic remarks on the way to class she struck me verbally, and said that if that didn't work she would do it physically. She was fed up with being around someone who had everything and appreciated nothing. I don't think anyone had ever spoken to me that way in my life. A physical blow would have been redundant. It was one of the greatest gifts I would receive.

Several months later, on my twentieth birthday, Carm gave me the same gift, but in a different package. She made me a collage, which I have next to me now. Over scenes of ocean, forest, cities, and a painting reminiscent of the Mona Lisa is pasted the following text:

> LIFE IS TOO DA
> MN SHORT
> THICK JUICY EXTRA
> VAGANT FLAVOR
> JUICY TOO DAM
> N RICH I MEAN
> FOR NEGATIVES SEE
> SO I SAVOR VALUE
> EVERY SINGLE SUP
> PLE SIMPLE DELICIO
> US INSTANT AS A
> PERSONAL SUPER
> LUXURIOUS PRECI
> OUS UNRAINCHECK
> ABLE GIFT—

Thirty-five years later, almost to the day, this is one of my holy texts, canonized by the passage of time and the experiences of life in this world. And as I reflect on it now, I was able to hear my friend Carm's admonition because I had the greatest respect for her. She was smart, caring, and although she didn't know that I knew, someone who quietly bore tremendous chronic physical pain. And I knew she cared about me as a person. So when those words came, they struck deep and opened my eyes to my unconscious lack of gratitude. And although stunned into speechlessness, I knew they came from love, they came from a person who lived with chronic pain, they were absolutely on target, and they weren't a personal attack. And those are the keys to admonishing sinners: love as motivation, a deep sense of one's own frailty, clarity about the issue, and demonstrated *unconditional regard* for the person admonished.

Although it is challenging to practice effectively, this spiritual work of mercy can have profound consequences. The effects on the one admonished were illustrated in my anecdote. But there also can be significance for the admonisher's daily devotional practice. When reading or praying over texts that describe Jesus' treatment of sinners, or the nature of sin, I discover a depth or nuance that I hadn't seen before. And I begin to grow more conscious of the depth and subtlety of my own sinfulness, which may blossom into the *tariki* of a light. Or as I see the effect of my compassionate correction on another person, I may receive the grace of feeling God's unconditional love for me. These deepened insights into self, sinfulness, and God's love I can then take back into my daily life, incarnating what I have received in an even more effective way. I become a better servant of the work. And this pattern, noted above, applies to the practice of all the works of mercy described in this chapter—both corporal and spiritual.

2. Instruct the Ignorant

In admonishing sinners, we speak to a person's *will*, the name the Catholic tradition gives to that part of us that desires and chooses. In instructing the ignorant, we speak to a person's *intellect* and *reason*. We seek to supply information or correct misinformation. The keys here are to have the correct information and know the developmental level of the other person. Again, a personal example may be instructive. When my daughter was six, she came to me with a question. "Daddy, where is God?" Being the theologian that I am, I said, "Well Anna, God is everywhere." She immediately began to look around, obviously without satisfaction—correct information, but poor analysis of developmental level.

Another experience I've had, a more positive example of instructing the ignorant, is teaching "adolescent atheists." In fact, I was one myself. Typically, bright young high school or college students unconsciously outgrow an image of God developmentally appropriate for a preteen (big, older, white hair and beard and robe, crown, throne, clouds, with circling angels; king in the sky on a throne), and don't have a more sophisticated concept with which to replace it. What then happens is that their education in science and their ability for abstract thought come together in the realization that the literal reality of such a being in such a place is impossible. And because they have identified this childish image of God with the reality of God, their logical conclusion is that there is no God. So they tell themselves that they are atheists.

The way I instruct such students is to tell them a story. I tell them that one day a young woman came to me and asked me if I believed in God. My reply was to ask her what she meant by God. She was incredulous. "Dr. Steele, you teach theology. You know, God, our great Lord and King in heaven, surrounded by angels." She meant it literally. My reply stunned her. I said, "Absolutely not." She presumed that I was rejecting the existence of God, when in fact I was simply rejecting her *concept* of God. That led to a wonderful conversation about the difference between an idea or image or concept of something, and the actual reality. As the semanticist Alfred Korzybski put it, "A map is not the territory it represents." My young student was able to begin to realize that she had identified the map with the territory, a particular image of God with the reality of God.

Now when my adolescent atheists hear this story, I usually see a light go off. They realize that it's possible they've made a mistake, and have thrown the reality of God out when they were only really rejecting a particular image of God. And at this point I typically make use of the pedagogical advice of James Marion, who maintains that we can:

...assist teenagers by introducing them to the rational arguments for God's existence that have been made by the philosophers. But even more importantly, we can help them by telling them that the God who lives deep within themselves is much more magnificent than the sky God they are now leaving behind. Within themselves, if they go deep enough, they will find a totally nonjudgmental, loving, and merciful God, a God who does indeed know how many hairs we have on our heads and about the fall of every sparrow (Matt. 10:29–30), and a God who, in fact, runs this universe from A to Z, human free will notwithstanding.[2]

Thus what are necessary for effective practice of this spiritual work of mercy are the tools of the gifted teacher: knowledge of the subject matter and one's audience. These can be gained through life experience, spiritual practice, and education. The typical effect on the instructor is Socratic wisdom. We come to appreciate how little we do know about our faith, and are compelled to learn more. This will in turn enhance our instruction. And we can then view any reading or study done in this regard under the category of spiritual reading. We can make our study our prayer, our spiritual practice.

3. Counsel the Doubtful

Doubt is an uncomfortable state of mind or heart characterized by uncertainty. One's thoughts or feelings are divided, rendering one paralyzed. In some cases the division is strictly intellectual or strictly emotional, and in others the mind says one thing and the heart another. And it is a condition we all know.

The first step in assisting a person who is troubled by doubt, and in fact the first step in all of the spiritual works of mercy, is empathy. We need to enter their condition, to stand with them where they are. That does not mean we consciously choose to doubt some truth of faith, or our own life choices. It simply means that we remember our own moments of doubt, and know how the other person must feel. We must speak and listen from where they are.

The second step is what psychologist Carl Rogers called *unconditional positive regard*. We create an emotional space wherein the other person feels loved and accepted unconditionally, even as a doubter. Who hasn't gone for advice to someone and been told either that doubting is wrong, or been told exactly what they should do? My typical response, when I'm the doubter, is anger or retreat. But when I'm in the presence of someone whom I sense understands where I am, and to whom I can say anything without fear of judgment or rejection, my spirit expands.

The third step in counseling the doubtful is to presume that the other person, under the guidance of God, will find the answer. Our role is to facilitate, to be a channel of grace. And in that role, a basic knowledge of what the Jesuit tradition calls *discernment of spirits* is most valuable. Most concisely, discernment is the process of sifting or sorting the various moods, feelings, thoughts, desires, and other interior movements of my soul into two categories: those from God and those not from God. Then I seek to mortify those not from God, and follow the promptings of those that are from God. But how do I know which is which?

A key biblical text is found in the fifth chapter of Paul's letter to the Galatians. In it the apostle makes a distinction between what he calls the *flesh* and the *spirit.* These are not to be understood as synonyms for *body* and *soul,* but as two impulses within us: one from God and one not from God. We can recognize those impulses that don't come from God, the "works of the flesh," as those that lead to: "fornication, impurity, licentiousness, idolatry, sorcery, enmities, strife, jealousy, anger, quarrels, dissensions, factions, envy, drunkenness, carousing, and things like these" (Gal 5:19–21). The impulses proceeding from God, the "fruits of the Spirit," are: "love, joy, peace, patience, kindness, generosity, faithfulness, gentleness, and self-control" (Gal 5:22–23). Discernment of spirits involves becoming conscious of my interior spirits, distinguishing those from God and those not from God, and gradually following the lead of the former and letting go of the latter.

One of the critical Jesuit insights into this spiritual practice of discovering God's will in my life is that the conjunction of the spirits of joy and peace are clear signs of God's will. When I feel both together in reference to a particular course of action, I can be confident that this is the direction God favors. So in the ministry of counseling the doubtful, what I can do is to listen for these spirits in what the other person has to say, or lead the person to their presence in their life. The other key is to accept the Jesuit insights that God typically works slowly, and that undue haste or urge to act quickly or abruptly is not from God.

The benefit to the one counseled is obvious, but what about to counselor? When I listen to another person's doubts and seek to facilitate discernment, I am strengthening my own ability to discern. And when I come to my daily spiritual practice, often while coming to quiet, I become increasingly conscious of the manifestation of the flesh and spirit within myself. And I become conscious of them in a situation where I am simply watching them, and not reacting. I begin to become conscious of the motives behind my actions in time enough to make a conscious choice. Is this flesh or spirit speaking to me? Should I follow its prompting or not? In other words, I learn to itch before I scratch. I gain more space or time to choose, more freedom. I can then bring this increased sensitivity and freedom into my daily life, and be a better counselor, a better servant of the work.

To sum up, my role as counselor is to provide an empathic, unconditionally accepting space for the other person, and facilitate their recognition of the workings of God's Spirit in their daily life, and in the dividedness they are experiencing. And to remember that it is God's Spirit that leads to faith (opposite of doubt), not my own brilliant wisdom.

4. Comfort the Sorrowful

To illustrate this work of mercy, I'll use a personal story. The occasion was dinner with a friend, Chris, whom I had not seen in over a year. We had a great conversation, and more importantly, we renewed our friendship. Two days later I learned that his father had died suddenly the day after our dinner. I wrote him a note and sent him a Mass card.

Several months later we were together again. When he first saw me, Chris came over and while shaking my hand and thanking me, said, "Your father died not too long ago too, didn't he?" I just nodded, and while looking into each other's eyes, our grips tightened. We were both comforted knowing that someone else knew exactly how we felt, that someone else shared our experience, that we weren't alone in our loneliness and pain.

But I noticed something else that night. Other friends, who had not lost their fathers, had great difficulty talking to Chris. And I knew why. What could they say, not having been through the loss he had, not sharing his condition? And perhaps even deeper, was the common human desire to avoid pain. For to comfort the sorrowful Chris, they would have had to enter his condition, at least in their imagination or with their emotions. And that would have been painful. That would have involved thinking about mortality and feeling another person's pain, instead of enjoying the anticipated pleasures of a Friday night out. And who, down deep, really wants that?

When I reflected on all this, something that Mother Teresa of Calcutta wrote years ago came immediately into my memory. She had been asked why she found it necessary to live with the poor and share their suffering in order to help them. She replied:

> Without our suffering, our work would be just social work, very good and helpful, but it would not be the work of Jesus Christ, not part of the Redemption. Jesus wanted to help by sharing our life, our loneliness, our agony, our death. Only by being one with us has he redeemed us.[3]

Mother Teresa saw Jesus as the one who was and is willing to share our condition, to be one with us in all that it is to be human. And the Apostle Paul in his letter to the Philippians tells us what Jesus gives up to do that. He gives up the nature of God, empties himself *(kenosis),* to enter our condition:

> Christ Jesus,
> who, though he was in the form of God,
> did not regard equality with God
> as something to be exploited,
> but emptied himself,
> taking the form of a slave,
> being born in human likeness.
> And being found in human form,
> he humbled himself
> and became obedient to the point of death—
> even death on a cross. (Phil 2:5b–8)

Now, Mother Teresa went on to say:

> We are allowed to do the same thing as
> our Lord; we are called to leave all that we
> have to share the desolation of the poor
> people, not only their material poverty,
> but their spiritual destitution, just as Jesus
> did. We are allowed to share in his work
> of Redemption, to be co-redeemers, by
> being one with the poor.[4]

Mother Teresa saw Jesus' *kenosis,* his emptying and dying
for us, as a call to each of us, a vocation, a vocation to be
co-redeemers, a vocation to enter the condition of the poor
and serve them within it. But the poor in our lives may not
be the materially poor. Our call may be to enter other
forms of poverty. Chris had not lost his job or his home.
He had lost his father.

5. Bear Wrongs Patiently

This is a difficult work of mercy to understand and
practice. To begin with, understanding what a *wrong* is, is
critical. Sidney Callahan, in her *With All Our Heart and
Mind,* distinguishes it from *sin* and *injury,*

> ...the other negative things that we must
> cope with in the traditional list of the spir-
> itual works of mercy. As compared to
> injury or sin, a wrong seems more gen-
> eral, less specific, less intentional, less

often directed with premeditated malice toward a particular individual. The time framework is also different, in that wrongs often are long-term chronic conditions as compared to acute attacks or brief episodes. A wrong is more socially institutionalized and impersonal.[5]

As a Catholic growing up in the South Carolina Piedmont in the mid-twentieth century, I learned that I would never be able to enter the stratosphere of local society. That was reserved for Presbyterians and Episcopalians. But as a Caucasian, I participated in the "wronging" of all African Americans in my functionally apartheid social structure. I was conscious of being wronged as a Catholic, but until the rise of the Civil Rights movement and Martin Luther King, I simply presumed the "separate-but-equal" school system, separate seating in public transportation and buildings, separate churches and mortuaries and restaurants and bars for blacks and whites, and even drinking fountains and toilets, was just the way things were. I was both wronged and an oppressor.

So a *wrong* is an injustice that is hard to change quickly, and one that a person suffers most often as a member of some group (e.g., Muslim, gay, woman, unemployed, elderly, etc.). And the deep hurt in this is in not being seen and treated as a unique individual. One is prejudged, stereotyped.

Now what does it mean to bear this patiently? Well first of all, it doesn't mean to accept an injustice, to say that it is a good thing or that it should not be rectified. To bear something means to carry something to a destination. Now the destination for an injustice should be its dissolution. What is implicit here is that a wrong will have to be borne until it is terminated. So the real question is what is the best way to bear a wrong until its destruction?

The key word is *patience,* a very difficult word for Americans. To once again quote Callahan:

> America has always been the land of ideal supermen who run faster than a speeding bullet. We are the people who wish to hurry up everything and provide instant relief, in medication, in fast food, in the fast-track career. At the same time we are programmed *not* to stand for wrongs, or as one state motto warns, "Don't Tread on Me." If you do, you will be instantly sorry. We won't tolerate delay, obstacles, or oppression—"Give me liberty or give me death," right this second. [6]

We have seen this clearly in the American response to the attacks of September 11, 2001. Patience is highly countercultural. But it is also the best approach to chronic injustice. Let me explain.

Two groups stigmatized by my generation of Southern white males as we grew up were blacks and gays. Now being a Catholic, and part of a family who saw any type of prejudice as wrong, mitigated the effect of the larger culture on me to some extent. But I was shaped by it.

Imagine my surprise when I walked into my freshman literature course at Notre Dame to find that the instructor was an African American woman. In many ways it was a fearful situation for me, because I had no experience of being in a subordinate position to a black person, and as soon as I opened my mouth in class my geographical origin was clear. This was 1968, just after the assassination of Martin Luther King in the south by a white southerner. Would I be placed in the category of a white racist simply because of my accent?

What I discovered was that my professor was an incredibly literate, kind, objective person. She was patient with me as a student, and most encouraging, unlike my white male teacher who very pointedly spoke down to the small group of St. Mary's women in our Japanese history class. Notre Dame was still an all-male school at the time, and the only reason the women were in our class was that it was a prerequisite for the sophomore year-in-Japan program that we were all a part of. The two classes together deepened my sensitivity to prejudice, and helped me escape at least the unconscious influence of my Southern upbringing.

When it came to stereotyping gays, the story is even simpler. Three years after graduation from college, one of my college friends called to tell me he finally had the courage to tell those closest to him that he was gay. I can't say I was taken completely by surprise, but what I can say is that I discovered that it had no effect on how I felt about him or our relationship.

In both cases, my literature instructor and friend must have each felt the weight of prejudice for most of their lives. But the way they had carried it, with patience, made it possible for me to see beyond race and sexual orientation to the unique wonderful people they each were. And once I learned that great lesson from them, I was able to apply it in many other situations. So their patience in bearing wrongs had a powerful effect on me. And as I reflect on it, it must also have had an important role in allowing them to grow as persons while feeling the weight of conscious and unconscious prejudice. And when I bring this reflection into my own *lectio divina* on the letter of James, I finally have some sense of why he said:

> My brothers and sisters, whenever you face trials of any kind, consider it nothing but joy, because you know that the testing of your faith produces endurance; and let endurance have its full effect, so that you may be mature and complete, lacking in nothing. (Jas 1:2–4)

6. Forgive All Injuries

According to Sidney Callahan, upon whom I draw heavily in this section, an *injury* is some harm or injustice directed at me personally. Its essence is the

> ...negative psychological intention or motivation on the part of the injurer. Intended malice or evil directed toward our person produces the real injury.... Real injuries are those acts aimed at us, as specific known persons, alive and operating in the world in this particular time and place. The perpetuators personally intended, or did not prevent when they could have, the particular harm inflicted on us.[7]

We each have been injured in our lives. And we know that the harm may be physical, emotional, psychological (self-esteem, sense of safety, personal integrity), or spiritual (doubt, loss of religious faith). And as Callahan observes, the degree of injury seems to be a function of how close it comes to the center of my person or to those whom I cherish (children, parents, friends), and the degree of intimacy I have with the one who injures me. A public attack on my character, an injury to a child, or an infidelity by a spouse are examples of the deepest hurts.[8]

There are three typical responses to injury, according to Callahan. The first is the deep spontaneous urge to strike back, to retaliate in kind, to seek revenge.[9] A second is to be overwhelmed and ultimately to blame myself for the attack.[10] A third is denial—we can't believe someone would consciously want to hurt us, so we find some way to explain it away: The person is having a bad day, or is the product of a dysfunctional family.[11] Note that forgiving is not a typical response.

None of these responses are good. The problem with denial is that we can't or won't see what is really happening. We fail to recognize the injury we have sustained, which prevents healing. And we fail to assign responsibility to the person who has harmed us, which lets them off the hook. The problem with being overwhelmed is that we ultimately participate in our own victimization by seeing ourselves as weak or helpless. And although retaliation feels good, it typically starts a pattern of increasing hostility that may bring harm to an increasing number of people. It also puts us in the role of injurer.

By choosing to forgive I avoid these very human but ultimately destructive responses. That is beneficial to self and others. But somehow it's not emotionally helpful. Why should I forgive someone who has harmed me? And especially when they could care less?

The first step in answering this question is to assert that to forgive does not mean to condone the act, or to say that it didn't happen, or that I was not injured. What it does mean is that I allow myself to feel the hurt to its depths,[12] but choose not to allow it to destroy my self-esteem nor change my character nor provoke an act of violence. This is the practice of discernment. Even though the other person seeks to hurt me, I *choose* to will the good for them. Regardless of how I *feel* about them. That's what Jesus meant when he told us to love our enemies. Love is willing the good of the other, regardless of how I feel about them.

So how do I forgive injuries? The first step is to acknowledge that I have been hurt,[13] and to be clear about the consequences: physical, emotional, social, psychological, and spiritual. The second step is to identify my first response: urge to retaliate, urge to hide or run away or accept the injury, or denial. The third step is to ask God for help[14] to overcome the desire to retaliate, or for restoration of self-esteem and the grace of courage, or to remove the blinders from my eyes so that I can see clearly what has happened and not deny my injury or my attacker's responsibility. I then ask God for the grace to forgive the one who has hurt me, and consciously pray for their healing or well-being. The fourth step is to do whatever is necessary for my personal healing. And finally, there should be an appropriate confrontation with my attacker, with the aim of restoration of a healthy relationship. Obviously, in certain cases (e.g., spousal abuse and rape), this may not be possible.

In many cases, forgiving those who have injured us leads to reconciliation. In cases where it doesn't, it promotes personal growth. And in either case it can lead to deeper appreciation of many scriptural texts in our devotional practice. We begin to truly appreciate the depth of Jesus' forgiveness of those who put him to death, and what the following text says about God and our deepest vocation:

> "You have heard that it was said, 'You shall love your neighbor and hate your enemy.' But I say to you, Love your ene-

mies and pray for those who persecute you, so that you may be children of your Father in heaven; for he makes his sun rise on the evil and on the good, and sends rain on the righteous and on the unrighteous. For if you love those who love you, what reward do you have? Do not even the tax collectors do the same? And if you greet only your brothers and sisters, what more are you doing than others? Do not even the Gentiles do the same? Be perfect, therefore, as your heavenly Father is perfect." (Matt 5:43–48)

7. Pray for the Living and the Dead

I grew up praying for others. I did it every night before sleep, every Sunday at Mass, and, once I started parochial school, every day during morning prayers and noon Angelus. But somewhere along the way I stopped. Likely it was during my adolescent self-worship. When I returned home to my faith during a particularly difficult spring semester junior year in college, the prayer that was most attractive to me was the contemplative tradition of the Trappists, a group I anticipated joining after graduation. I wanted to swim in the experience of God that I had just begun to feel. Intercessory prayer seemed unsophisticated, a childish attempt to influence God rather than becoming more intimate with God. And over the intervening thirty years, such prayer has not been a major part of my spiritual life. Part of the reason is that I've always presumed God knows better than I what is good for others and me. Perhaps another part of it is that my life has been relatively easy, allowing me the illusion that I'm in control.

So what has changed my mind, and led me to a revaluing of this form of prayer? Well, it's a combination of things. First, it's those life events that make me wish I'd chosen the Trappists instead of "life in the world." Had I been a Trappist, there would have been only two parents' deaths to mourn instead of four, and that of my step-mother-in-law. And I would not be intimately connected to the various struggles and sorrows of my wife, children, and now grandson; a connection so deep that I have on a number of occasions tried to bargain with God to let me carry their pain instead of watching it. And had I been a Trappist I would not have to deal with the backbreaking "straws" (one more bill to pay, call to make, engine light coming on just after the car returns from the shop, colleague to placate), that come to us all. And personal bad habits and addictions likely would have been identified and purified had I been a Trappist for three decades. To put it more abstractly, the life I have chosen has presented me with situations and events and people that have clearly demonstrated that my intelligence, social skills, bank account, and will power are insufficient to insure the security and well-being and happiness of myself and those I love. And it has been just these situations that have pushed me to intercessory prayer.

But why has it taken these people and circumstances to get me to pray to God for help? Why do I have to be in foxhole situations before I reach out? I am reminded of what Jesuit Walter Ciszek wrote concerning just such a situation in his own life:

> ...the greatest grace God can give such a person (speaking of someone who trusts in their own strength exclusively) is to send him or her a trial they cannot bear with their own powers—and then sustain them with His grace....[15]

So it's really about recognizing and admitting, deep down, that "I can't do this, I can't find the answer, I don't know what to do or where to go." I have to recognize and admit weakness. And I hate that.

But as I reflect back over my personal foxhole experiences, I recognize that when I have reached out to God from my weakness and insufficiency, an answer has always come. When I reach out to God for something I need for myself, I gain insight into the issue, or a sense that I am unconditionally supported by God, or in many uncanny cases, I gain what I need from a coincidental call from a long-lost friend, or an unexpected gift, or a randomly chosen book. When it comes to praying for a troubled relationship, by opening myself to my own weakness and the need for a higher power I am led to greater sensitivity, and this has often transformed the relationship. In other cases I have had insights that seem to come from nowhere (lights, angelic influence, *tariki*) and, when offered to others, have proven helpful. So intercessory prayer in general has either helped me personally, or has allowed God's help to flow through me to others. It has been good for me, and when I have prayed for insight and compassion in order to help others, it has gone beyond self-benefit.

But what about people with whom I don't have direct contact, distant in place or time, living or dead? Can my prayer on their behalf have an actual effect? To answer I once again turn to the wisdom of Sidney Callahan. She says that to accept the efficacy of intercessory prayer on behalf of others, we have to presume two things. The first is that we are all connected at a deep level, a theological presumption presented earlier as the communion of saints. The second is the distancing of God from Creation that allows us the freedom of choice. Then, as Callahan puts it:

> We can imagine that God is all around and throughout Creation but separated and self-limiting enough so that separate human wills and actions will be free to make a real difference. God's noncoercive policy may mean that only human beings can freely invite and freely open their own human sphere to God's active power. God constantly broods over the Creation and is seeded within each human being. God longs to be invited to help. To ask is already to find. God is everywhere, but freely initiated human cooperation seems necessary to focus, activate, and magnify the divine force of love and power.

Intercessory prayer can (thus) be seen as operating like a magnifying glass that can focus and intensify God's light upon a particular point. Another image...is that of a magnet that enters and changes the magnetic fields and so attracts God's power to a particular event....Images of water are also used. Prayer for others can be seen as an opening of flood gates or providing new channels of irrigation so a parched terrain can be watered with God's love and power. One wishes to bathe and renew another in the living waters, giving them drink and refreshment.[16]

With these beautiful images in mind, I now have a way of understanding what my prayer on behalf of others might do. And although there is no empirical proof of its efficacy, at a minimum it sensitizes me to the needs of others and encourages me to experience myself as part of the communion of saints, the mystical body of Christ. This in turn leads me to a deepened *lectio divina* of Paul's writings. In Romans he says, "For as in one body we have many members, and not all the members have the same function, so we, who are many, are one body in Christ, and individually we are members one of another" (Rom 12:4–5). And in his letter to the Ephesians he tells us we should

grow up in every way into him who is the head, into Christ, from whom the whole body, joined and knit together by every ligament with which it is equipped, as each part is working properly, promotes the body's growth in building itself up in love. (4:15–16)

So now I really begin to see that, from the standpoint of the Catholic spiritual tradition, every thought, word, prayer, and deed has an effect. The effect may be on myself, on another person, or on the entire mystical body. No work of mercy, however small or hidden, is lost. And this certainly includes intercessory prayer. As Callahan puts it:

> The intercessory prayer of the individual and the Church may well be co-creating and co-redeeming the evolving universe. Teilhard de Chardin had such an understanding of human initiative, as have many poets and creative spirits. I love Annie Dillard's idea that each act of artistic creation and each act of ordering done by a human being, whether seen by another or not, helps create and sustain the universe.[17]

Conclusion

The corporal and spiritual works of mercy are the traditional ways the Catholic spiritual tradition has embodied love of neighbor. They are each calls to really hear and live the words of Jesus, who told us that we can love and serve God by loving and serving others. This is not to de-emphasize the interior spiritual practices described in the earlier chapters. It is simply to suggest that the interior graces received in spiritual reading, *lectio divina*, Ignatian mental prayer, the Rosary, and the liturgy, can be shared. In that sharing these gifts are multiplied, both within us and between us. The mystical body of Christ is built up, the communion of saints made even more intimate. And when we bring the fruits of these works back into our daily interior and communal spiritual practice, our prayer is strengthened: *jiriki, tariki,* incarnation; deeper *jiriki,* deeper *tariki,* more effective incarnation.

APPENDIX
A Guide to the Rosary Beads

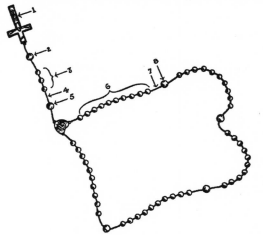

The Rosary is the most popular of Marian devotions. The pattern of meditation in the Rosary focuses on the *mysteries* (events in the lives of Jesus and Mary).

To Say the Rosary

1. Make the sign of the cross and say the Apostles' Creed while holding the crucifix/cross at the end of the rosary beads.

2. Say the Our Father on the first large bead after the crucifix/cross.
3. Say three Hail Marys, one on each small bead following the first large bead.
4. Say the Glory Be.
5. Announce the First Mystery; then say the Our Father on the large bead.
6. Say ten Hail Marys.
7. Say the Glory Be.
8. Announce the Second Mystery; then say the Our Father on the next large bead.
9. Repeat steps 6 and 7.

If you'd like to use the pattern of meditating on the traditional mysteries, there are four clusters: 1. the Joyful Mysteries, 2. the Luminous Mysteries, 3. the Sorrowful Mysteries, and 4. the Glorious Mysteries. You can use any cluster you want, but often people use the Joyful on Mondays and Saturdays and Sundays during Advent, the Luminous on Thursdays, the Sorrowful on Tuesdays and Fridays and Sundays during Lent, and the Glorious on Wednesdays and Sundays.

These are the mysteries, with a text from scripture (where available) to help you identify what they are:

The Joyful Mysteries

1. The Annunciation (Luke 1:26–38)
2. The Visitation (Luke 1:39–56)
3. The Nativity (Luke 2:1–20)

4. The Presentation of the Child Jesus in the Temple (Luke 2:22–39)
5. The Finding of the Child Jesus in the Temple (Luke 2:41–52)

The Luminous Mysteries

1. Jesus' Baptism in the Jordan (Matt 3:13–17)
2. Jesus' Self-Manifestation at the Wedding of Cana (John 2:1–12)
3. Jesus' Proclamation of the Kingdom of God with His Call to Conversion (Mark 1:15)
4. The Transfiguration (Luke 9:28–35)
5. The Institution of the Eucharist, as the Sacramental Expression of the Paschal Mystery (Mark 14:22–25)

The Sorrowful Mysteries

1. The Agony in the Garden (Matt 26:36–46)
2. The Scourging at the Pillar (John 19:1)
3. The Crowning with Thorns (John 19:2–6)
4. The Carrying of the Cross (John 19:16–17)
5. The Crucifixion and Death of Our Lord (John 19:18–30)

The Glorious Mysteries

1. The Resurrection (Matthew 28:1–10)
2. The Ascension (Acts 1:1–11)
3. The Descent of the Holy Spirit (Acts 2:1–42)

4. The Assumption of Mary
5. The Crowning of Mary as Queen of Heaven

The Prayers Used in the Rosary

The Apostles' Creed

I believe in God, the Father almighty,
   creator of heaven and earth.
I believe in Jesus Christ, his only Son, our Lord.
   He was conceived by the power of the Holy
      Spirit
   and born of the Virgin Mary.
He suffered under Pontius Pilate,
   was crucified, died, and was buried.
He descended into hell.
On the third day he rose again.
He ascended into heaven,
   and is seated at the right hand of the Father.
He will come again to judge the living and the
      dead.
I believe in the Holy Spirit,
   the holy catholic Church,
   the communion of saints,
   the forgiveness of sins,
   the resurrection of the body,
   and the life everlasting. Amen.

Our Father (The Lord's Prayer)

Our Father who art in heaven, hallowed be thy name. Thy kingdom come. Thy will be done on earth, as it is in heaven. Give us this day our daily bread, and forgive us our trespasses, as we forgive those who trespass against us, and lead us not into temptation, but deliver us from evil. Amen.

Hail Mary

Hail Mary, full of grace, the Lord is with thee; blessed art thou among women, and blessed is the fruit of thy womb, Jesus. Holy Mary, Mother of God, pray for us sinners, now and at the hour of our death. Amen.

Glory Be

Glory be to the Father, and to the Son, and to the Holy Spirit. As it was in the beginning, is now, and ever shall be, world without end. Amen.

Notes

Introduction

1. Madeleine L'Engle, *Walking on Water: Reflections on Faith and Art* (New York: North Point Press, 1995), 58.

2. Ibid., 18, 23–24.

3. Ibid., 194.

4. Thomas Merton, in Janice Elsheimer, *The Creative Call* (Colorado Springs, CO: WaterBrook Press, 2001), 4.

Chapter One

1. Michael Casey, *Sacred Reading: The Ancient Art of Lectio Divina* (Liguori, MO: Liguori Publications, 1996), 18.

2. Thelma Hall, *Too Deep for Words: Rediscovering Lectio Divina* (New York: Paulist Press, 1988), 9.

3. Thomas H. Green, *Opening to God: A Guide to Prayer* (Notre Dame, IN: Ave Maria Press, 1977).

Chapter Two

1. www.monksofadoration.org/rosarywd.html.

2. www.christendom-awake.org/pages/dmiller/beads&prayers.htm.

3. www.vatican.va/holy_father/john_paul_ii/apost _letters/documents/hf_jp-ii_apl_20021016_rosarium-virginis-mariae_en.html.

4. Ibid., 22.

5. Robert Frost, "The Road Not Taken," in *The Complete Poems of Robert Frost 1949* (New York: Henry Holt and Company, 1949), 131.

6. Walter J. Ciszek, *He Leadeth Me* (San Francisco: Ignatius Press, 1995), 158.

7. John Paul II, ibid., 9.

8. Raymond J. Gunzel, *The Treasures of God: Unlocking Our Spiritual Heritage* (Notre Dame, IN: Ave Maria Press, 2002), 117.

Chapter Five

1. International Commission on English in the Liturgy (ICEL), Eucharistic Prayer IV, in *Roman Missal* (Washington, DC: USCCB, 1973).

2. David Loy, "Jesus and Buddha as Stories," http://www.bpf.org/tsangha/loy-jesusbuddha.html.

3. Joseph M. Champlin, *The Mystery and Meaning of the Mass* (New York, Crossroad, 1999), 44.

4. Joseph Ratzinger, *The Spirit of the Liturgy* (San Francisco: Ignatius Press, 2000), 88.

5. Ibid., 216–17.

6. Champlin, 42.

7. Ibid., 69.

8. Ibid., 86.

9. Jean Corbon, *The Wellspring of Worship* (New York: Paulist Press, 1988), 35.

10. Ibid., 39, 41.

11. Ratzinger, 212.

12. Champlin, 106.

13. Ibid., 113.

14. Ratzinger, 90.

15. Ibid., 175.

Chapter Six

1. Mitch Finley, *The Corporal & Spiritual Works of Mercy: Living Christian Love and Compassion* (Liguori, MO: Liguori Publications, 2003), 8.

2. James Marion, *Putting on the Mind of Christ: The Inner Work of Christian Spirituality* (Charlottesville, VA: Hampton Roads Publishing Company, Inc., 2000), 56.

3. Malcolm Muggeridge, *Something Beautiful for God: Mother Teresa of Calcutta* (San Francisco: Harper & Row, 1971), 67–68.

4. Ibid., 68.

5. Sidney Callahan, *With All Our Heart and Mind: The Spiritual Works of Mercy in a Psychological Age* (New York: Crossroad, 1990), 123.

6. Ibid., 121–22.
7. Ibid., 146.
8. Ibid., 148–50.
9. Ibid., 142–43.
10. Ibid., 150–51.
11. Ibid., 153–54.
12. Ibid., 153.
13. Ibid., 147.
14. Ibid., 161–62.
15. Ciszek, 71.
16. Callahan, 183–85.
17. Ibid., 184.

Bibliography

Print

Callahan, Sidney. *With All Our Heart and Mind: The Spiritual Works of Mercy in a Psychological Age.* New York: Crossroad, 1990.

Casey, Michael. *Sacred Reading: The Ancient Art of Lectio Divina.* Liguori, MO: Liguori Publications, 1996.

Champlin, Joseph M. *The Mystery and Meaning of the Mass.* New York: Crossroad, 1999.

Ciszek, Walter J. *He Leadeth Me.* San Francisco: Ignatius Press, 1995.

Corbon, Jean. *The Wellspring of Worship.* New York: Paulist Press, 1988.

Finley, Mitch. *The Corporal & Spiritual Works of Mercy: Living Christian Love and Compassion.* Liguori, MO: Liguori Publications, 2003.

Frost, Robert. "The Road Not Taken," in *The Complete Poems of Robert Frost 1949*. New York: Herder, 1949.

Green, Thomas H. *Opening to God: A Guide to Prayer*. Notre Dame, IN: Ave Maria Press, 1977.

Gunzel, Raymond J. *The Treasures of God: Unlocking Our Spiritual Heritage*. Notre Dame, IN: Ave Maria Press, 2002.

Hall, Thelma. *Too Deep For Words: Rediscovering Lectio Divina*. New York: Paulist Press, 1988.

International Commission on English in the Liturgy (ICEL). Eucharistic Prayer IV, in *Roman Missal*. Washington, DC: USCCB, 1973.

L'Engle, Madeleine. *Walking on Water: Reflections on Faith and Art*. New York: North Point Press, 1995.

Marion, James. *Putting on the Mind of Christ: The Inner Work of Christian Spirituality*. Charlottesville, VA: Hampton Roads Publishing Company, Inc., 2000.

Merton, Thomas, in Janice Elsheimer, *The Creative Call*. Colorado Springs, CO: WaterBrook Press, 2001.

Muggeridge, Malcolm. *Something Beautiful for God: Mother Teresa of Calcutta*. San Francisco: HarperCollins, 1986.

Ratzinger, Joseph. *The Spirit of the Liturgy*. San Francisco: Ignatius, 2000.

Electronic

David Loy, "Jesus and Buddha as Stories" p. 1. http://
www.bpf.org/tsangha/loy-jesusbuddha.html.

www.christendom-awake.org/pages/dmiller/beads
&prayers.htm

www.monksofadoration.org/rosarywd.html

www.vatican.va/holy_father/john_paul_ii/apost_letters/
documents/hf_jp-ii_apl_20021016_rosarium-
virginis-mariae_en.html

ILLUMINATIONBOOKS

Other Books in the Series

Hear the Just Word & Live It
by Walter J. Burghardt, S.J.

The Love That Keeps Us Sane
by Marc Foley, O.C.D.

The Threefold Way of Saint Francis
by Murray Bodo, O.F.M.

Everyday Virtues
by John W. Crossin, O.S.F.S.

The Mysteries of Light
by Roland J. Faley, T.O.R.

Healing Mysteries
by Adrian Gibbons Koester

Carrying the Cross with Christ
by Rev. Joseph T. Sullivan

Saintly Deacons
by Deacon Owen F. Cummings